DISCOVERY
OF THE
WORLD

DISCOVERY OF THE WORLD

A Political Awakening
in the Shadow of
Mussolini

Luciana Castellina

Translated by Patrick Camiller

VERSO
London • New York

This English-language edition published by Verso 2014
Translation © Patrick Camiller 2014
First published as *La scoperta del mondo*
© nottetempo srl 2011

The moral rights of the authors have been asserted

1 3 5 7 9 10 8 6 4 2

Verso
UK: 6 Meard Street, London W1F 0EG
US: 20 Jay Street, Suite 1010, Brooklyn, NY 11201
www.versobooks.com

Verso is the imprint of New Left Books

ISBN-13: 978-1-78168-286-9 (HBK)
eISBN-13: 978-1-78168-287-6 (US)
eISBN-13: 978-1-78168-659-1 (UK)

British Library Cataloguing in Publication Data
A catalogue record for this book is available from the British Library

Library of Congress Cataloging-in-Publication Data
A catalog record for this book is available from the Library of Congress

Typeset in Electra by MJ & N Gavan, Truro, Cornwall
Printed in the US by Maple Press

It is a great bore to keep a diary but a great delight to have kept one.
                    The Diary of John Ruskin, 30 December 1840

CONTENTS

FOREWORD

Fourteen years old in 1943. My mother, a girl, is tottering towards adulthood in a world that suddenly shows itself to be larger and more intricate than the one she has learned about on the cramped, stifling school benches of Fascist Italy. The narrative begins on the Adriatic in Summer 1943, at the Mussolini Villa in Riccione. A tennis match with the dictator's daughter, Anna Maria, is interrupted by security men in plainclothes. During the night Mussolini is arrested in Rome: the Fascist regime is crumbling. From 1943 to 1947, the years of the diary, a succession of momentous events breaks up the normal rhythm of life: the Armistice, the capitulation of a ruling class that is no longer felt to represent anyone, the German occupation, the Resistance, the end of the war, the great issues of the peace.

The diary unfolds on two tracks. The first, typical of a teenager, is an introspective search for an identity of her own. The second is a gradually dawning awareness of everything beyond the self: the war, racial persecution, the end of an era, and then a peacetime world with broader horizons (Paris, Prague, Europe) and a society more complex, unjust and unequal than she has glimpsed from the bourgeois vantage point of her childhood.

As in all coming-of-age stories, the pages tell of a will to shake off the confines of an over-familiar environment, to be a player in life and no longer just a spectator. This is a microhistory of discovery, in which the author overcomes fears and hesitations to embrace life in its entirety and to assume her own part as a being alive within it.

In essence it could be the trajectory of any fourteen-year-old. But the historical circumstances are clearly exceptional: they speed up the learning process and lead to choices which, in another time, might have been different for a girl from a middle-class family. In some respects so normal, loving the festivals and holiday camps that she attends between Cortina and Venice and knowing that – partly because her family is after all modern and unprejudiced – life is about pleasure as well as duty, she nevertheless feels an urgent need to commit herself to a collective enterprise. It seems the natural course to take in those years between 1943 and 1947, when the discovery of life mingles with a growing understanding of the plight of deportees, with the suffering in the family caused by the death of Aunt Vittorina fleeing racial persecution, and with the experience of aerial bombardment and widespread fear. On the one hand, there are the intellectual circles she begins to frequent in Rome, her growing interest in painting, her trip to Paris, the great modern metropolis, and her encounters (in Paris, Milan and Venice) with a more sophisticated world than the one she has previously known. On the other hand, slightly later, there are the numerous acquaintances she makes between Prague and Yugoslavia, with young people from different social and geographical backgrounds to whom she feels joined in a common endeavour to rebuild the world on new foundations. I see this journey of my mother's as an initiation into life rather than politics – a discovery of the world in its complexity, and of the possibility of fully engaging with it.

The diary closes in 1947, but the final pages of the book allude to what came after. My mother, like so many other young Italians of bourgeois origin at that time, had become a Communist in order to build the world anew after the devastation of war. But instead the world closed again and split into two – an outcome sealed by the electoral defeat of the Left in 1948.

In my own childhood, between the late Fifties and the Sixties, the world shrank once more and society grew more divided: the only ones who counted were the Communists; the rest were 'others'. Yet for me it was a land of the seven wonders. We were different, and proud of it; indeed, my younger brother and I found it unthinkable that the central purpose of our lives should not be to make society more just. We did not live in a ghetto, however. At home all kinds of people came visiting: legendary leaders such as Togliatti; other Communist intellectuals who had opted for political activism; and a wide variety of 'fellow travellers' who were felt to be less close, being from countries where the Communist Party had not been able to win over intellectuals as it had in Italy. They talked and argued at great length about ideas, politics, art and literature, with no distinction between their public activity and private life. I have always felt that my parents enjoyed themselves; there was nothing bigoted in this single-minded commitment of theirs. Communist intellectuals of the postwar generation were not 'fanatical' like the older ones about whom my mother writes in her diary. They represented an Italian version of the modern, progressive, cosmopolitan bourgeoisie. The nature of their politics is understandable, precisely because the discrediting of the Italian ruling class under Fascism meant that progress could not but involve a radical orientation.

My political convictions as an adult have become very unlike those of my mother, but I understand why her diary ends on a note of nostalgia for that life in the Communist Party. From those years of sharp political conflict, when Italy was growing richer yet remained deeply divided, I remember a great optimism, a great faith in progress, and a constant attempt to keep abreast of society. As a child, I would accompany my mother to so many meetings, leafleting expeditions and lunches with 'the comrades' in various regional organizations. I saw a country I would not have seen otherwise, and I came to realize that the ways in which people live and work are different, that their social background matters and can weigh heavily against them. It was a real education.

My own fourteenth birthday came twenty-five years after my mother's, in August 1968. That too was a moment of passage: it marked the close of the postwar period and the end of my childhood. I did not keep a diary, but I sometimes ask myself what I would have written in one during the years between the movement of '68 and the rise of terrorism in 1973. Like my mother before me, I was too young to be an out-and-out protagonist, but of course I took part confusedly in events that would have a lasting impact. Italy has certainly changed a great deal since then – from a basically agrarian country into a major industrial power – and the movement of the late 1960s was itself symptomatic of the transformations and the emergence of new social strata. In a sense, my 'baby boom' generation was more fortunate, living as it did through the affluent society, a huge expansion of education, the legalization of divorce and abortion, and new opportunities for women. But we also experienced greater disappointment. I too, like my mother, wanted to understand Italy and the world, to be an active participant in the events of the time. In fact, I left Rome in 1973 and went to study in Northern Italy, because it seemed to me that something very important was happening in that more developed part of the country. But there is not the same note of optimism in my recollections of the period: I simply felt trapped and needed to get away. In the 1970s I sensed that outside Italy – the Italy of terrorism, Moro's assassination, and conflicts that were tearing society apart yet offered no convincing alternative models or values – there was a wider world to be discovered and won. I do not know if I was right to leave my country for the United States: it was my answer to the sense of suffocation that Italy provoked in me during those years. Nor do I know whether my mother would have done the same if she had been born in the 1950s instead of 1929. What is certain is that the idea of a wider world to be understood and experienced came with her stories of railway construction in Yugoslavia, with her opening of our house to people from every corner of the globe, with all the languages she spoke, and with the cosmopolitan sensibility that she developed in the postwar Communist movement but which had its essential roots in her Central European family.

My path in life has been individual, and I do not think that my generation shared the certainties of the previous one (or parts of the previous one) about what could be achieved together. I think we were more fortunate, but less happy.

Someone suggested that the title of this book should have been 'Happiness'. For what is happiness if not perception of the humanist truth that, although you are an individual and can make choices, life has meaning only if you are part of something greater, if you discover that you can decide to participate and to be yourself within the collective? I think that my mother's diary is the story of that discovery.

Lucrezia Reichlin

ACKNOWLEDGEMENTS

When I recently came across the diary I kept as a teenage girl between 1943 and 1948, I thought it might be worthwhile to share the memories it contains with my grandchildren Alfredo, Fushu and Vito, so that they would have some idea of what it meant to be their age in the distant 1940s, when nothing could be taken for granted and a whole world was waiting to be discovered.

Such is the origin of this book, which is based on my diary from those years. My own two children are closer to the experience of which it tells: Lucrezia has expressed her point of view in the foreword, while Pietro will communicate his undoubtedly severe assessment to me in a very private form.

I would like to thank Ginevra Bompiani for her decision to publish the book, thereby allowing me to reach out beyond the family to a number of others born in the 1990s.

1. WAR

It must have been about seven in the evening. In July it is still light at that time, although the shadows of the pine forest around us had begun to lengthen. I remember them falling on the tennis court as Anna Maria and I played balls inexpertly over the net. She had once had polio and found it difficult to run.

Then a plainclothesman called her over and abruptly put an end to the rally, without any explanation. All she said to me was 'I have to leave right away.' And she vanished behind the policeman, whose job it had always been to watch over her and her younger brother Romano.

Anna Maria was Anna Maria Mussolini, daughter of Benito and Rachele, my classmate at primary school and the first two years of secondary school: 1940–41 and 1941–42. I had moved to Verona for the third year, 1942–43, but we met up again in the summer at Riccione, where our game was so rudely interrupted. Her father had been arrested during the day in Rome: 'detained at the Podgora barracks in Trastevere' – for 'his own protection', it was later announced, almost apologetically.

Only late that night did I understand what lay behind Anna Maria's mysterious farewell. I found the others – mostly friends of

1

my cousin Paoletta and therefore quite a bit older than me – in front of Hotel Vienna, where our group used to meet to play table tennis in the gardens. Not yet fourteen, I scarcely ever managed to get a word in edgeways. But this time they listened to me as I began to speak of Villa Mussolini – and of my sense that the sudden end to our game of tennis must have meant something.

EIAR, the state radio network, announced that Il Duce had been arrested after dark.

The next day, cutters sailing out at sea unfurled their bunting – to celebrate, the adults told me. On little fishing boats moored offshore, groups of holidaymakers sang the old national anthem – Mameli's *Hymn*, no less – together with various songs from the First World War, also 'to celebrate'. And at lunchtime, in the place where we were boarding, tagliatelle made from rare white flour unexpectedly arrived on the table. 'To celebrate,' the Romagna waitress repeated, in a discreet whisper of complicity.

This, at the age of fourteen, was my initiation into politics – so important that on the same day, 26 July 1943, I began to keep a 'political diary', as I wrote by way of a title. I used the back pages of an old exercise book set aside for *cronache*: that is, the Italian compositions cultivated in secondary schools such as the Collegio degli Angeli in Verona, the city where I had been obliged to live for family reasons. One of these notebooks, from a few months earlier, bore the title: 'The *Alpini* Are Returning.' It was a reference to the elite mountain combat troops of the Julia Division, who 'fought valiantly in Russia and marched for long distances on the snowy steppes, and who now parade with their flags and dirty, ragged standards, testifying to the enemy's frenzy and to Italian valour. We have our hands outstretched in a Roman salute.'

This diary, closely written in a series of notebooks until Autumn

1947, is the source on which I shall draw to reconstruct the stages of my early political development – a piece of history covering a small part of my generation, born in the late Twenties to early Thirties.

26 JULY 1943

I discover a host of things on the first day of the post-Fascist era.

First of all, bewilderment: the Fascist regime was the only context I had when I reached the age of reason; no one gave me a glimpse of any other, except by saying that the war – which by that summer had engulfed half the world – was leading Italy to disaster. Like everyone else of my age, I felt completely at a loss.

I also discovered a patriotic spirit, no less. I wrote that it was awakening, because 'it had dozed off in all Italians under the command of a man who was leading their Fatherland to ruin' (always with a capital 'F'). After all, 'since I am and was anti-Fascist, I wished in spite of myself that the English would come to Italy and liberate us from the Germans – in short, that we would lose the war'. Now, however, I was sure that the war would be won, 'because we are fighting for the House of Savoy'. I even added a *Viva l'Italia!*

The war had to be won, therefore. Yet I felt sick when I learned that peace had not broken out.

'The 26th is a Monday and there are no newspapers. So we still don't know much. But at one o'clock we all ran to the radio. What will they say? This is Radio News … Bulletin 1157 … The Supreme Command … In Sicily … There is some change of form, but the content is the same as ever. And then Badoglio's pronouncement: firmness before all else; no outbursts of enthusiasm, no demonstrations; they are out of place at a moment when all the forces of the nation must be strained for victory. "Italy", the communiqué further explains to citizens, "stays true to its promise, jealously guarding its age-old tradition". End of broadcast', I note with disappointment, having recorded the text in my diary. (Later, in the tent on the beach, it is rumoured that Senator Morgagni – president, I'm told, of the Stefani news agency, precursor of today's ANSA – has shot himself.)

'We all feel a bit let down. No peace around the corner, the Germans still in our home.' Indeed, the war will now last even longer, since 'if the two Italian divisions that surrendered in Sicily without a fight had known that Mussolini would no longer be head of government the next day, they would have made themselves martyrs simply so as not to give in.' And I add: 'I'm an Italian, after all, and I know what Italians are like.'

27 JULY 1943

On 27 July, still in Riccione, I encounter militant anti-Fascism for the first time. I come across it in the town centre, reconnoitring a long way from the seaside on my bicycle. In front of the Casa del Fascio, the Fascist Party headquarters, a crowd is cheering on those who have climbed the façade and are stripping away its decorative sheaves with pickaxes. There is a lot of tension in the air, and 'I don't think their intentions are good'.

The following day, the papers announce that 'any demonstrations will be dispersed without warning, by gunfire'. The circular 'issued by General Roatta, head of the General Staff, orders that "ringleaders and instigators of disorders who are caught red-handed will be summarily shot" and that "any soldiers who side with them will be immediately put before a firing squad". What will happen to the people I saw on the walls of the Casa del Fascio in Riccione?'

But the resort area in Riccione remains calm. In the tent we discuss at length the fate of the fatherland and its links with the ongoing war. In the evening, though, we go to see the swashbuckling adventure film released earlier that year: *Il figlio del corsaro rosso*, with Luisa Ferida.

Amid the war and the air raids, a holiday is still a holiday – unusual though it is, at least for me. I am without my family, alone with my elder cousin, and not at the Venice Lido (where I have spent every previous summer) but in this unfamiliar place called Riccione. Suddenly it has begun to seem more interesting than I thought – a thoroughly modern seaside resort, a million miles from the old-world atmosphere of the Hotel des Bains in Venice. The beach does not have cabins, but striped tents. And further away a new institution: the holiday camp, with its skinny children from the poverty-stricken rural hinterland of Emiglia Romagna.

Very close to our tent are a group of boys from Rome with whom I immediately fall in love – with all of them. I am not yet fourteen and look no more than twelve, so not one takes any notice of me. But it is enough for me to be in their sphere of influence.

The Zurlini brothers, full of themselves and with the air of people in the know, look at us with a certain commiseration. Sixteen years later, watching *L'estate violenta* at the cinema, I realized that the director, Valerio Zurlini, had been among the group in the neighbouring tent – and that the plot of the film, down to the finer details, was based on our summer in Riccione and Zurlini's love (the subject of much whispering) for a war widow much older than himself. The scene with the Allied air raid of 29 July on Bologna railway station – which catches Jean-Louis Trintignant (Valerio) and Eleonora Rossi Drago (the war widow) on the run and impels her to hurry back to her child in Riccione – also struck a chord in my cousin and me. After the fall of Mussolini, sure though we were that any fears were exaggerated, we had reluctantly obeyed instructions from home to break off our holiday without delay. So we too had found ourselves at the country's most important railway junction on that fateful day, escaping but not knowing where to seek shelter, shut up in an immobilized train carriage as the sirens wailed and people shouted and cried around us.

THE 1930s

My political formation up to 25 July 1943 had followed two con-tradictory lines, but these had run in parallel without creating any friction. One was the Riccardo Graziola Lante della Rovere ele-mentary school, in Via Tevere; the other was my family.

My wonderful hyper-Fascist schoolmistress, Giralda Giraldi Caricati, decorated our classroom walls with large coloured-chalk tableaux depicting the glories of the regime: the imperial conquests, the draining of the Pontine Marshes south of Rome, the annexa-tion of Albania and installation of Victor Emmanuel III as its king. The dates of my 'composition' notebooks always have the letter 'A' after them (for *anno*, 'year'), followed by Roman numerals indicat-ing the age of the 'Era Fascista' (EF for short). So, on 18 October 1939 A XVII EF – my last year in elementary school – I write: 'On 28 October 1922 an army of Blackshirts marched on Rome under the command of Il Duce. After this event the Fascist government, saviour of Italy, gave a vigorous impulse to agriculture by reclaim-ing the Pontine Marshes.'

The marshes feature again a few days later, since in that region 'Il Duce has established a new commune, Pomezia'. Meanwhile, thanks to 'the valour of our great Condottiero, another 1,800 families are leaving to work the fertile land in Libya'. On 31 October I express gratitude for another 'purely Fascist invention of Arnaldo Mussolini [brother of Benito]: the savings campaign, whose great day is just now being celebrated'. On 8 November 1939 A XVII EF, I write enthusiastically about our headmaster, 'who came to speak to us of the famous latifundia of the ancient Romans; they did not cultivate the fields and so the plebs remained without work. But Fascism has put an end to that wretchedness.' (I would never have thought that in 2010 Italy's main literary prize, the Premio Strega, would be awarded to a book about the epic deeds of those distant times: Antonio Pennacchi's *Canale Mussolini*.)

The great novelty, repeatedly discussed in these 'compositions', is the school radio – a kind of loudspeaker attached to the wall above the teacher's desk, which tells us every day of some new development. On 17 November it records the fourth anniversary of the criminal sanctions that 'a coalition of fifty-two nations against Italy' inflicted on us; on 18 November it commemorates 'the war against the Empire of the Negus', and I write that the Abyssinians are 'fierce soldiers, but the Italian soldiers were very courageous because the example of Il Duce inspired them with confidence'; on 10 February it is the turn of the Conciliation Treaty of 1929, 'the work of two towering minds: Pius XI and Mussolini'; and on 8 April we are reminded of the conquest of Albania, where Italy, 'as in all places, has been spreading civilization'. 'Since it is washed by the Mediterranean – which, as Il Duce said, should again be called Mare Nostrum – Albania had to rejoin its Italian mother country.'

The notebook containing these literary exercises has a map of the Empire on its cover beneath a large letter 'M', together with my membership number (125008) of the Fascist youth organization, the Gioventù Italiana del Littorio (GIL). For them I receive the highest final grade: 'praiseworthy'. The next year, 1940–41, I therefore move on with nearly all my old classmates to 1A of the Torquato Tasso secondary school.

The Bottai reforms have meanwhile replaced 'grades' with two categories of 'judgment' – on school performance and on 'membership and activity in the GIL'. And the judgment on my first term is already that I am not 'very conscientious at the GIL musters'.

This cannot be a symptom of rebellious anti-Fascism, however, since in the second term my 'activity at the musters has improved'. And I have risen from the rank and file of the 'Little Italians' to the elite units clad in sailor suits, which anyone attending the chic Caio Duilio school in Lungotevere Flaminio joins as a matter of course. I have even been appointed drummer, and that activity I remember enjoying immensely. (After all these years, I can still play the drum reasonably well.)

Anna Maria Mussolini was again in our class, after a long sick leave due to polio, and it was everyone's ambition to be invited to play the usual children's games in the afternoon at the Villa Torlonia (Mussolini's state residence from the 1920s on). I was among the privileged few, and on one occasion I even caught sight of Il Duce at the door. We almost never crossed the threshold ourselves, but I remember thinking that the house was furnished appallingly.

We would remain in the gardens, where 'Donna' Rachele (Mussolini's wife) sometimes put in an appearance. Here we had all a child could wish for: tree platforms, huts in the bushes, all kinds of games. Anna Maria had only to ask and a host of attendants would deliver. We did miss an afternoon snack, though: at five o'clock the police guards would bring something for Anna Maria and Romano, but not for their guests. It was beyond my mother's comprehension that Il Duce's family could be so badly brought up. After all, were they not from Emilia Romagna, noted for the generosity of its people? To this day I still cannot really fathom it. The children were in the charge of policemen, who obviously had orders to bring them a bite to eat. There was no provision for us.

But our entertainment did stretch to films – indeed, it was at Villa Torlonia that I first discovered the cinema. At the far end of the gardens, near Via Spallanzani, there was a projection room where the Mussolinis went to see films provided by the official Istituto Luce. The Cinecittà studios and the Centro Sperimentale di Cinematografia (the national film school) had been created a short time before, and the cinema in general was part and parcel of the Fascist regime. That detached building, which witnessed my initiation into the seventh art, was actually the headquarters of the International Educational Cinematic Institute – a great honour for our country, despite the breaking of the link with the League of Nations on which it had originally depended. It continued to function and to show European citizens, including in the democratic countries, how educational activities should be organized. What we did not know was that in the interstices of these institutions, and of the journal *Cinema* (edited by the elder brother of my tennis partner, Vittorio), many future Communists were taking the first steps in their career. We were too young to understand that there was an ambiguity in Fascism, and therefore some reason to feel attracted by that modernizing, anti-bourgeois dimension which found expression in Futurism. Such penchants of the 'blackshirted revolutionaries' traversed the intellectual circle around Bottai's *Primato*, but certainly not our classrooms filled with the most provincial rhetoric.

The ambiguity did not last long, however, even for the grown-ups. As they later recounted, the mask fell with General Franco's landing in Spain and the support he immediately received from Mussolini.

ANNA MARIA

Anna Maria was arrogant but *simpatica*. Fully aware of the power that came from being Il Duce's daughter, she used it to terrorize our poor Italian and Latin teacher Mr Gianni, a gentle figure who, like all his colleagues, was forced to wear in his buttonhole a badge saying: 'God curse the English!' And this was despite the fact that the director of Tasso College, Professor Amante, boasted of treating the Mussolini children no differently from everyone else. Once he had even made Romano sit his exams again in October – an event that acquired legendary status.

Anyway, Mr Gianni did not trust his superior's declarations and, just in case, he preferred to give Anna Maria consistently high marks. Impudent as she was, she would stand up straight, point to the girl sitting beside her and ask: '*Professore*, why did I get marked excellent and she unsatisfactory, when I simply copied her home-work?' And when the class was caught rioting during a teacher's absence, she always confessed with a touch of irony to being the one responsible for it: 'It was me, *professore*.'

The worst moment for Mr Gianni came at one o'clock, on those occasions when the class was prolonged and we had to get to our feet to listen to the War Bulletin. Anna Maria loved to comment aloud on the news, referring to things she had heard at home. So we knew that, when coffee was banned, the Mussolinis had already laid in sizeable stocks; and we were regularly informed that her father considered King Victor Emmanuel III to be a cretin.

The later course of events could not but strengthen this judgment on the monarch. Anna Maria spoke of him when I met her again shortly after the end of the war, at the home of a former classmate who had remained close to her because her mother had been a Fascist activist. (In fact, she was later interned at Coltano, the camp that held those accused of trying to rebuild a party inspired by Fascist ideals, the future Movimento Sociale Italiano.) 'My father', Anna Maria told me, 'was overthrown because he trusted that cretin of a king.'

It was the first time I had seen her since that interrupted tennis match. I knew by then that she had been taken from Riccione that same evening, together with her brother Romano and her mother, to Rocca delle Camminate, the little castle not far from the Mussolinis' former residence in Predappio. Clearly her father had intended to join them there, 'once the ire of the people from my Romagna has been placated', as he put it in a letter to his sister Edvige shortly after his arrest.

Meanwhile two years had passed, and so many things had happened. It was a sad encounter: I never set eyes on her again. She died years later of a heart attack, still quite a young woman.

PREWAR EDUCATION

It was precisely because of those afternoons at Villa Torlonia that I discovered my family's anti-Fascism. The guards who checked our names at the sentry box did not fail to point out that there was something not quite right about me: my father was not a registered Party member. At first they didn't even want to let me in, and although they eventually agreed, in view of Anna Maria's insistence, they continued to look at me askance.

11

It was not that Father had refused the famous membership card out of firm political convictions. Since his work did not depend on the state – he was a sales representative – he could afford to steer clear of any action that appeared to him unseemly. To my great amazement, however, beloved Uncle Memmo – my mother's brother and, like her, 'mixed' (that is, half-Jewish) – was forced to change his surname to that of his Aryan mother: a Liebman from Trieste became a Marzi from Tarquinia. He was an office worker at the Banca Nazionale del Lavoro, and a refusal on his part would have meant losing his job.

More consciously anti-Fascist was my mother's intended, Nino Salis, who used to come visiting at Via Serpieri, where we had been living with my grandmother after my parents separated, when I was four years old. Nino became her legitimate husband only after a real obstacle race that lasted a good eight years. First it was necessary for the Liebman–Castellina marriage to be annulled by the Apostolic Tribunal of the Sacred Roman Rota, a mysterious body that I heard people link to the Pope's brother, the lawyer Pacelli, who had to be paid huge sums to meet the fees of a never-ending process. After five years, a ruling finally came down that the marriage between Mother and Father had never taken place – which puzzled me for a long time, since I didn't understand how I could have been born in that case. But then new race laws again made it impossible for the two 'intended' (as they liked to call themselves) to become man and wife: a 'mixed race' woman could not marry an Aryan man, because the Italian race would be polluted by such a union. They then tried the solution of a *non concorditario* religious wedding, allowed under the agreement of 1929 between the Pope and the Italian government, but without combining it with the parallel civil ceremony. Though anomalous, the church ceremony might thus have sufficed to legitimize the entry of the eternal fiancé into a house where he would not otherwise have been able to reside.

Once more, the devil put a spanner in the works. A priest willing to act as their accomplice had been found in Sardinia, because my future stepfather came from Sassari. But on the day before the wedding was due to take place, the island was declared a war zone, and anyone like my mother who had not been born in Sardinia was banned from travelling there.

Providence relented, however, just as all hope seemed to have run out. Another man, by the name of Le Pera, now entered the scene and fuelled my curiosity for the next few years: he offered to arrange the obscure and expensive, but ultimately successful, solution of 'Aryanization', which was the preserve of a number of specialist Fascist lawyers. Thus, in May 1942 the wedding finally took place in the church of San Bellarmino on Piazza Ungheria. Kneeling at the altar, Mother kept turning round to blow me a kiss, evidently worried about how I would react to an event that was unheard of at the time.

A fortnight later Nino Salis, husband of the 'annulled' Lisetta Liebman, was called up despite his advanced age of forty-three – not to the front, but for service as a lawyer at the military tribunal in Verona. All of us, including my grandmother, moved there with him, because in 1942 it was thought that the war might well last some time longer.

I loved my stepfather Nino, as I did my real father, although the two could not have been more different. He introduced a much more robust hostility to the regime into our family – which, despite the Jewish blood from Trieste flowing through its veins, scarcely ever talked of Fascism and anti-Fascism. Not that it did nothing – good heavens, no. The very idea of underground opposition was unthinkable, but it is true that the legendary bookseller Tombolini, then working at the Modernissima store on Via della Mercede, managed to get hold of forbidden books from Paris and calmly placed them on the shelves. I gradually began to leaf through them, although what I read and what I heard about them at home did not clash in the slightest with my school lessons or the little pearls I used to write about Il Duce, the Paludian marshes and the Abyssinians, or even with the endless jokes about Fascist officials whispered at convivial gatherings (above all, bridge evenings) in the solid Roman middle classes to which we belonged.

In any event, Receipt No. 1622, issued on 23 January 1936 by Linda Varese on behalf of Baroness Nolli di Tollo, testifies that such anti-Fascism did not prevent Mother from donating a couple of gold wrist buttons to the fatherland – although in fact I was the real donor. I well remember when I went with Mother (who threw her old gold wedding ring into the brazier) to the Altar of the Unknown Soldier and handed over my contribution to the colonial conquests that the other colonial powers wished to deny us.

A WINTER IN VERONA

Verona – the city to which we followed Nino Salis after he was called up in 1942 – made a huge impact on me. It was there that I began to understand a few more things about the shape of Italy. Both Rome and Venice (where we used to spend the summer) seemed part of a different century once I had discovered the bigotry and conservatism of provincial Veneto.

I enrolled in the third class of a public secondary school, like Il Tasso in Rome, and on the first day the schoolmistress called the register and asked the new pupils why they had come there. I stood up, white as a sheet, and explained that my mother's husband had been summoned to join the army in Verona. The witless teacher gave a smile of commiseration, then insisted on asking me whether that meant my real father was dead. Pierced by rows of sheep-like eyes bulging with amazement, I grew ever paler and had no choice but to relate the story about the Sacra Rota and the annulment. I would have found it easier to say I was a murderer's daughter. The next morning, I refused to go back to school and shut myself away at home for days.

In the end they solved the problem by sending me to a rather select college for young noble ladies, Agli Angeli, originally founded by Napoleon and now attended by girls whose family wealth made them more worldly. No one asked me a thing about the Sacra Rota, for example. But the fact remains that I knew I was different from the others, having undergone special experiences and acquired a much greater knowledge of life. I did not find this disagreeable and, since the young Veronese ladies were loyal to the regime, I felt bound to consider myself a little anti-Fascist.

The Guf cinema* played a role in this, as it did for many others. I received permission to go to the Saturday afternoon screenings at this large cinema on Stradone San Fermo, some way from the city centre. I knew no one there: the rest of the audience was much older than me. But I saw some fantastic films which, though Fascist, made me realize that the world was much more complicated than I thought. The ones that made the greatest impression on me were *Noi vivi* and *Addio Kira*, both starring Fosco Giachetti and Alida Valli: he as a GPU (pre-KGB) agent who eventually commits suicide, she

---

* Gioventù Universitario Fascista: the Fascist organization to which all university students were required to belong.

as a Russian who ends up a milkwoman in the Ottakring district of Vienna.

I think it was at the Guf cinema in Verona that I first heard the words 'Soviet Union' and 'Communist'. And, despite all the film-makers' efforts to make them fit wartime propaganda, I became interested in what lay behind the two terms.

The only other film I recall is *The Golden City*, with Kristina Söderbaum – a fierce denunciation of class injustice made at the UFA studios in Berlin. But the reason why this has stuck in my memory cannot have been fortuitous: nearly fifty years later I happened to find out that the manager of the Guf cinema had joined the partisans after 8 September 1943 and died fighting a few days before the Liberation.

The war, far away in Rome, became more palpable in the city on the Adige; it was there that I experienced death at close quarters, in a personalized way. One day our fine and sensitive literature teacher, who had never asked me what I was doing in Verona, returned from a brief absence pale in the face and dressed in black. She had been officially told what she had suspected for a long time: her brother, a lieutenant in the Italian Army in Russia (ARMIR), would never be coming home. He had died in the desperate retreat through the snowy plains of Russia and Ukraine – a region we knew well because the Napoleonic epic was the object of particular attention at the Agli Angeli college, and the drama of the crossing of the Berezina in 1812 was more present to us than the fate of the Italian troops scattered on the eastern front in the winter of '42–'43.

Then there were the Caioli brothers, children of Grandmother's great friend Annetta, in whose country house, L'Apparita, at Castiglion Fiorentino, we would spend a few days every year. There were three of them, each tall and handsome, and seven or eight years older than me. Marcello, the youngest and most likeable, was killed in Yugoslavia, while Giovanni, it was later discovered, died of typhus in a prison camp in India, having been captured in the first few days of the war and shipped there from East Africa. But we had no opportunity to commiserate with Annetta: she too died before we managed to see her again, travelling in a coach that came under machine-gun fire on her way back to L'Apparita.

'42–'43: MONTEVIALE

There were air raids in Verona, and the sirens wailed more and more often at night. I was sent to Monteviale for my safety.

Monteviale was one of the mythical places of my childhood. My Ascoli aunt and uncle from Venice had some land in that village ten kilometres from Vicenza, on a hill facing Monte Berico, and we would go there every year between the end of August and the beginning of the school year (which was very late in that period). The days were long and empty, giving me time for that priceless boredom which today's children no longer enjoy. You need time on your hands if you are to think, to explore your surroundings, to get to know the flora and fauna – and to talk with country people different from yourself. We harvested the grapes and trampled them in wooden vats, growing heady from the perfume of the must.

I even made my first communion there, together with my cousin of the same age, Luciano Ascoli. We prepared for it with exclusive catechism lessons from the parish priest, Don Girolamo Fortuna; this was an unusual privilege, as indeed was the holding of the actual ceremony in the autumn. Bruno, the brother of our maid Palmira who had followed us from Monteviale to Rome, played the

'Serenata Messicana' on the organ – a piece then much in fashion. It was a bold choice in a village where the priest had banned Saturday evening dances, even though such impropriety was permitted elsewhere in the vicinity. But no one other than us realized that it was not a sacred song.

Bruno was a fine pianist, but that was one of the last times he played a keyboard instrument. He lost an arm at the Fornace, the factory in the plain where nearly all the young men of Monteviale worked. That was how I learned that there were such things as work accidents.

Don Girolamo was a jovial and likeable man, whose black, violet-fringed habit (like those of all priests in the Veneto) was always spotted with stains. He often came to dinner, and we youngsters used to laugh because anyone could see from a mile that he was in love with Aunt Vittorina. Now and then, in his cups, he would lower his head and mutter: 'Lord, what a beautiful woman!'

The war entered people's lives in Monteviale at the beginning of the Forties. The first symptom was joyful, when Giovanni Cisotto, one of the large family of tenant farmers who lived behind our house, sent word to his wife from his army post in Greece that the son she was expecting should be called Orfeo. This represented a new departure, because it was the habit of the Veneto peasantry at the time to give their children the same name as their master's (and, when something was said to them, to signal obedience by answering: 'Comandi'). Then news of the first deaths began to reach one family or another: from Africa, Yugoslavia and Russia.[*]

---

[*] The mythological name imposed by Orfeo's father in a courageous break with tradition did have a stimulating effect, however, since his son became one of the first to emigrate from Monteviale to the factories of Milan in the early 1950s.

When I arrived in Monteviale from Verona, in the winter of 1942, my Ascoli cousins, Paoletta and Luciano, had already been there since the beginning of the school year, and cycled every morning to the *liceo ginnasio* in Vicenza. They had been forced to evacuate after their house in Milan took a direct hit from a bomb.

In fact, they had moved to Milan only a few years earlier, when the race laws made it impossible for Uncle Renzo (a baptised Jew who had married my mother's sister Vittorina) to exercise his profession as a lawyer in such a small town as Venice. But until their home was destroyed in that air raid, life did not change very much for the Ascoli family. Although my cousins were 75 per cent Jewish (50 per cent on their father's side, 25 per cent on their mother's), they had been baptised and were able to attend school. My uncle, thanks to influential friends, worked for the legal department of the industrial firm SNIA Viscosa.

At home there was naturally talk of the war and the fact that it would end one day, but it was not clear to anyone how that would come about. No one even seemed to be planning for it.

When I arrived in Riccione in July 1943, my knowledge of the war came from the radio: Allied troops had landed in Sicily, but 'the enemy attack was being effectively contained by our valiant soldiers along a line running from Agrigento to the Plain of Catania'; in the East the Germans had repelled an offensive by 'strong Red forces' at Orel and in the Kuban and Donets regions. A number of things were obviously being hushed up; brothers, sons and husbands were already being mourned. But since no one close to us had officially been 'killed in action', the war remained an abstraction.

I knew that aircraft were dropping bombs on people's houses – in Rome too, though in an area some way from the centre, San Lorenzo, that I had never heard mentioned before. No one we knew had been hit. And in Verona, where bombs fell rather more often, the feverish descent into the basement was great fun.

I was also aware that race laws had been passed, but Jewish friends and relatives did not seem to have suffered a dramatic change in their lives, and so the racial persecution – which no one tried to explain to me – appeared strange and incomprehensible. It was serious above all because it had deprived Aunt Vittorina of the right to have a domestic servant. And, since my cousins' forced move to Milan, it had deprived me of summers at the Venice Lido.

In the pages of a diary that Mother kept for just a few months, between October 1938 and January 1939 (she was not the ruminative type but always looked ahead), there are some allusions to the persecution. She calls it 'an injustice', because it means 'attributing to Italian Jews the anti-Fascist feelings of foreign Jews'. There is a little more apprehension concerning 11 November, the 'inexorable date' when 'unheard-of restrictions' are to be announced, but again the only example she gives concerns the domestics. 'What a pain!' she adds. A little later, she does refer to the 'terrible things raging in Germany' and the fact that, according to a friend from Trieste, 'rich Jews [in Austria] are being allowed to leave on condition that they give up all their possessions'. There is no reference to poorer Jews, but it seems that Andrea Vivanti, the brother of her Venetian Jewish friend Margherita, had decided to sell up and go to Rome, spend everything and become a monk. (In the end, more realistically, he emigrated to Brazil.)

But on the race question, Mother's diary refers mainly to 'delight-ful little stories' that were doing the rounds: 'Farinacci* says the

---

* Roberto Farinacci (1892–1945): important Fascist leader before and during the Second World War, noted especially for his virulent anti-Semitism.

Jews are entirely to blame for the disputes in Europe. A voice interrupts and says: it's cyclists who are to blame. Someone asks: why cyclists? And he replies: why Jews?' Or: 'Do you know why Jews are no longer allowed into school? Because they pay fees for one and learn for ten.' Or another: 'Starace* is no longer called *segretario* [secretary] but only *tario*, because Segre is a Jewish name.' And the *tario* tells off 'the mayor of Caltanisetta because there isn't enough of a race campaign in his town. To which the mayor replies that it's true so would they please send him a couple of Jews.'

AUGUST 1943: CAVALESE

With the sudden return home from Riccione after 25 July, my diary breaks off on the very day I began it. It resumes on 10 August, and I re-read the lines dashed off a fortnight earlier: 'At those extraordinary moments, when I was glad I could sincerely wish for the victory I used to conjure away because of the Fascists ...' Now, however, I note that 'the Italian people have calmed down', because the reality has become glaringly evident to them: Fascism is no more, but in essence it is still there because it is a crime to denounce it. To me the only proof of its disappearance is the 'rebaptizing' of our ships: the destroyer *Black Shirt* is now called *Artillery*, and *Squadrista* [Fascist paramilitary] has become *Sea Rover*.

Above all, the war goes on – and it goes on alongside the Germans. I dig up a few commonplaces about them, having set these aside in the preceding years. They are our 'historic enemies, descendants of Barbarossa – barbarians who have always trampled

---

* Achille Starace (1889–1945): National Secretary of the Fascist Party from 1931 to 1939.

on the soil of our homeland, cruel and cold-blooded and therefore so different from Italians. There can never be an alliance between us and them.'

Nor do the English seem much better. (I speak little of the Americans; they must have seemed a distant people, little mentioned at school except to say that their country was discovered by an Italian.) During those weeks they were raining down bombs on Bolzano, Bologna and Turin – an act of cruelty not seen in 1915–18. Radio London, which we listened to secretly in search of news, informed us of virtually nothing other than the air raids, in a tone of satisfaction.

I wrote these disconsolate entries in Cavalese, a pleasant town in Trento province where I had been sent with my grandmother when the situation in Verona became too alarming. The military tribunal where my stepfather served was still functioning, now under the command of the Badoglio government, but no one understood what was taking shape. The unreal normality of this period was felt even in the muffled living-room of our house in Verona, a human refuge for the magistrates and court-appointed lawyers who worked with my stepfather, mostly without a family of their own in the city. They sensed the dangers of the situation, but they did not know how things would work out, and spoke gloomily to one another about what Marshal Badoglio ('too anti-Fascist') was likely to do. It was suggested that Ettore Muti, considered by many to be Mussolini's heir apparent, had not died accidentally while the Carabinieri were taking him under arrest to Fregene, but was deliberately killed because he was a top figure in the Fascist party and Badoglio feared that the king wanted to rely on him during the transition.

In the evenings there was also talk of one Bonomi and other

unknown anti-Fascists who had supposedly created some sort of committee.* Despite my stepfather's position, we did not learn even from him that 3,500 people were arrested for 'sedition' and ninety-five murdered by the forces of law and order during those forty-five days between the fall of Mussolini and the Armistice proclamation. In fact, neither before nor after 25 July did anything much happen at the Verona military tribunal: just some routine cases of petty theft and minor incidents in the army. Serious matters were obviously decided elsewhere, since the authorities did not trust the little group of middle-aged lawyers and magistrates who were neither Fascist nor anti-Fascist.

Life was so normal that, after returning from the sea, I was simply sent off on holiday again – although without Mother, who remained in Verona with her new husband. Grandmother and I took a lot of trunks with us, so that the family silverware, linen and valuable fittings could be kept safe from the bombs in the rented house in the mountains. (They were brought back two years later, after the end of the war.)

That summer in Cavalese passed like any other, and in the end my mind was distracted from politics because there seemed nothing for me to write about it. I did, however, note one announcement from the Royal Palace in my diary: 'Ninety days of national mourning for the deceased King Boris of Bulgaria'.

The diary skipped quite a lot of days that August. Although the last division of the Italian army meanwhile quit Sicily, the retreat did not really seem like one: it felt almost like a tactical withdrawal,

---

* Ivanoe Bonomi (1873–1951): Social Democrat politician, leader of the umbrella National Liberation Council formed in September 1943, and prime minister after the Allied entry into Rome the following year.

since the papers continued to speak of 'the effectiveness of the Italian–German armies'.

It was by roundabout means that I learned more about the Allied campaign in Sicily that was writing a new page in history. The brother of Aunt Norina, on my mother's side, was a career captain in the army there, and for a time alarming communications reached us through her. But then the South fell into a long silence as the occupied and liberated parts of Italy were cut off from each other.

Only after the Allies reached Rome, and we were reconnected to the South, did Aunt Norina finally manage to go to the Plain of Gela in Sicily, where the last traces of the army unit under Captain Mancia's command had vanished. She wandered the war-ravaged countryside looking for him among the dead, but there were too many corpses for each to be accounted for. Of Messina – I wrote in my diary after the Liberation – 'it is said that the bombing killed more people than the earthquake.' And to justify the distance I felt from the new allies, I recorded that General Eisenhower's soldiers made a cynical play on words: 'Messina is a mess.'

Some gossip in Cavalese talks about Radio London. But that too seems a dubious source, reporting mainly the 'good job' performed by the RAF. In mid-August it informs us that 2,000 tons of bombs have been dropped on Milan, and that the operation was 'a resounding success'. The holidaymakers/evacuees who tell me the news are distraught, since many of them come from the worst-hit cities of the North.

I understand more only when Zeno comes out of the blue to find me. I first met him the year before, on a day when my father, very unusually, took me with him to visit some friends or other who were spending their holidays in a Trentino resort not far from Cavalese. Although I had written to Zeno that I was staying near the village where his family had their summerhouse, I did not think that he would come looking for me.

But he does come. He is very tall, very handsome and sixteen years old, whereas I am only fourteen and my breasts have not yet developed. Above all, he knows a lot of things. I go down to the river with him and, sitting on a rock beside the water, listen enraptured as he talks of Badoglio, the Fascists, the anti-Fascists, the Germans, the king.

The passion for politics that flared up in me at Riccione and gradually died down for want of fuel now comes back to life. The pages of my diary are again filled with vague hagiographic reflections. And on 7 September I excitedly break off my thoughts of the day and write in big letters: 'Pietro Badaglio has asked for an armistice and this has been accepted. The war is over.'

That evening I report that I was noting down recent events when I suddenly had to switch to writing about the Armistice; 'perhaps I will read it again when many years have passed'. I first heard the news, without believing it, while I was out walking with a friend. Similar rumours had circulated several times before and no one attached much weight to them any longer, so we just continued with our walk. But once I was back home and had begun writing my diary, Grandmother rushed in and told me that the radio said the stories were true. EIAR had broadcast the announcement after playing 'Una strada nel bosco', a popular song of the time, as if to make people think it was an ordinary news item. I later found out that the Marshal's stentorian voice informing us of the Armistice was pre-recorded: both he and the entire Court had already headed for Brindisi to set up shop there.

My feelings were running high at the thought that peace was finally around the corner. Curiously, however, perhaps because of things I had learned from Zeno, I realized that the situation had also become more dangerous. I note in my diary something I heard the Germans say more than once: 'Lead for the enemy, gas for traitors.' Their revenge – I predict – 'will be terrible. And their bombing horrific, like with the English. The English and the Germans are all of a kind: inhuman beasts, without a shred of feeling.'

The tone, as one can see, is becoming ever more racist. But having spent many years at a school where my teacher wore a badge saying 'God curse the English!', and where history consisted of nothing other than a series of Teutonic invasions, I think this was not without justification.

My trust in Badoglio remains unchanged, perhaps because of his Italic race. It seems impossible that he has done such a thing – signed the Armistice – 'without reflecting on it for a long time and without reaching a decision fully in the interests of the fatherland'.

10 SEPTEMBER 1943

In the following days I have a chance to verify the Marshal's far-sighted solicitude.

In Cavalese nothing happens after the Armistice. Holidaymakers gather in the town square and discuss what to do. Some boys nearing military age run off who knows where.

Then the first soldiers from regiments stationed in the area begin to show up and to ask us for civilian clothes. They too want to melt away, but it is difficult for them since the South Tyroleans sided with the Germans and are not inclined to offer any help.

My point about the Alto Adigeans does not surprise me today. In my diary, recalling childhood holidays at Sesto di Pusteria, I mention that a South Tyrolean family lived near our rented house and that I used to play with Zita, a girl of my own age with long ginger pigtails and countless freckles. She knew some Italian because it was the compulsory language at school, but her parents spoke only German and spurned any attempt to communicate with them. 'Mother', I write in my diary, with incipient shame, 'was adamant about teaching Zita Italian and couldn't understand why she and her parents were so proud in refusing.' Only after the war did I understand that, for them, 8 September was the day of liberation – from the Italian occupation they had suffered since 1919.

After 8 September, however, the Germans did not show up in Cavalese. Nor, for that matter, did any other authority – we had no idea which it might be. Three days of waiting succeeded one another: communications with the outside world were cut; here and there gunfire could be heard in the distance. Then – it must have been around three in the afternoon – a Wehrmacht armoured car appeared in the square, together with an officer seated on a motorcycle and another in the sidecar. We were paralysed: now only women, children and old people. The officers got down, smirking contemptuously, walked into the bar and ordered a drink. I felt duty-bound to repeat the gesture of Il Balilla,* and, since I had learned German as a child from Fräulein governesses, I told them they were not wanted and should go away. There was an icy moment, then one of them pulled out his pistol, toyed with it for a moment and said: 'I'll forget that because you're just a

---

* Giovan Battista Perasso, affectionately known as Il Balilla, was a young popular hero in eighteenth-century Genoa, who sparked off an anti-Habsburg rebellion with an act of defiance towards an Austrian official.

kid. Go home.' And worried holidaymakers immediately took me home, where I was handed over to Grandmother and shut up indoors.

Thus ended my only contribution to the Resistance.

12 SEPTEMBER 1943: FLIGHT

The next day – the fourth since the Armistice declaration – the idea of remaining cooped up in a room seemed intolerable. So, on 12 September 1943, I became more adult than Grandmother: I told her that I wouldn't obey orders any more, that I'd go out and actually take charge of things. In the town square, the little group of holidaymakers had been informed that a train would be leaving tomorrow. Clearly we needed to travel on it, and that is what we did, having hidden our precious trunk in the cellar.

At Ora, where we had to change, a long freight train was parked on the tracks; the locomotive was pointed towards the Brenner Pass. All around, German soldiers were patrolling with rifles over their shoulders.

I didn't immediately realize what was going on, wrapped up as I was in my new responsibility as head of the family to check connections and to keep an eye on the luggage and Grandmother. Then, all of a sudden, I was struck by voices coming from the wagons and by arms stretching from the windows. They were Italian soldiers who had offered some resistance and were now being taken to concentration camps in Germany. They threw out little notes, perhaps with the address of their family, hoping that someone would pick them up and let their mother or wife know what had happened to them. But there was nothing we could do: the Germans prevented us from getting closer.

We left with aching hearts. When I think back today, I still feel a sense of guilt: it was as if we ran away.

In Verona, as our train was creeping at a snail's pace beneath the station roof, the nervous, jerky sound of sirens began to warn of an air raid. As a major railway junction, the city was constantly being targeted. But no one paid any attention, and before long we were home at last – or anyway in that provisional house, furnished the best way possible, with tables and chairs that Mother had found in a junk shop.

15 SEPTEMBER 1943: RETURN TO ROME

In fact, Mother was not happy to see us back. She'd have preferred us to remain in Cavalese, since there was a climate of fear and tension in Verona and no one knew what to do. The orderly, a farmer from Veneto, had cleared off as soon as the Armistice was announced. Meanwhile the raw officials at the military tribunal were not prepared for the idea of defection: they no longer went to the office, but nor did they run away.

The indecision could not last. I remember one wild evening when Nino's colleagues came to our house in dribs and drabs, as awkward as conspirators, determined not to keep playing along but incapable of opting for underground opposition. Fortunately the Germans and Fascists were too busy during those days to pay any attention, and so no one posed a threat to all those who, one by one, headed off south by various routes.

We women also left, hurriedly shutting up the house on Via Tezzone. I would not see it again: when I returned after the war to pick up my things, all I found was a hole filled with rubble.

As we prepared to take a train south, we had little idea of what was happening in Rome – partly because friends and relatives who had remained there also knew and understood little. Some news reached us about the clashes immediately after 8 September; they seemed to have led to some deaths, right in the Villa Borghese area that was so familiar to us. But since none of our own people was directly involved, the information was far from precise.

(No one told us even about the heavy fighting two days after the Armistice at Porta San Paolo and during the Battle of Montagnola, when improvised armed resistance to the Germans among the population in the Garbatella neighbourhood resulted in hundreds of casualties.)

The fact is that a concern with collective, political matters had not been much of a habit; everyone was too involved in sorting out their own problems. And there was fear.

Formally, there was an Italian government acting with authority from the runaway king; and Calvi di Bergolo, military commander of the city, opened executive sessions in the name of 'His Majesty', assisted by Victor Emmanuel's aide-de-camp, Colonel Montezemolo. Rome was called an 'open city' – an unclear but somehow reassuring term.

Although the Germans are in control, I write in my diary, 'the arrival of the Allies is expected from one moment to the next. They will probably land at Lido di Ostia, and General Caviglia, holding the municipal command though dependent on General Kesselring, is supposed to have said that they will arrive in a few weeks and he will go to meet them together with the Pope, flying the Vatican flag on their car.' We are told that the Blackshirts are back in the capital, though few in number.

Comforted by such prospects but in the dark about the fate of our relatives – they had gone south, alternating between the Adriatic and Tyrrhenian coastal routes to confuse anyone who might be in pursuit – our little group of females left too: Mother, Grandmother and myself, and Signora Labua, the wife of one of Nino's colleagues at the military tribunal.

We advanced towards Rome, but we did not know whether our crowded train would ever get there. At Bologna, between one air raid warning and another, we had to get off and climb up into different wagons. The stops became increasingly frequent, because our train had to make way for convoys heading north with whatever the Germans had managed to purloin. At the same time, transports piled high with weapons, armour and machine-guns passed us on their way south.

The station at Orte was in ruins. At Poggio Mirteto we saw flames leaping from fuel wagons that had been hit by a bomb; the fire spread to the whole hillside. It felt as if I was at the front, although I wasn't too sure what fronts were.

HOME AT LAST

At last I am back in my city, in a house where I'll remain for a good many years. But it is not the one I lived in before we went to Verona. It is the Salis family home on Via Vallisneri, behind the zoological gardens, which was reorganized after Mother married Nino to create room for all of us, and has not previously been occupied.

Rome seems almost normal: the only new feature is the women performing male roles as tram conductors, postal workers, street cleaners, and so on.

I am happy not to be in hated Verona, to be finding again the friends I have known for so long. The very day after my arrival I go with them to the Supercinema to see *I nostri sogni* [Our Dreams], with Vittorio de Sica and Maria Mercader.

Nino joins us a few days later, having taken a circuitous route in several stages so as not to arouse suspicions. An office has opened in Rome where soldiers can apply for leave. Should he go there or not? There is much discussion and hesitation, because the situation is changing by the day. Mussolini has been sprung from his prison at Gran Sasso, Calvi is under arrest, and Montezemolo has apparently managed to escape by the back door from the war ministry in Via XX Settembre.

Nino finally makes up his mind to file the application: he was born in 1900, after all, and should be on safe ground. We wait with bated breath for him to return home, but everything has gone well: they've granted him indefinite leave. But who granted it? The next day – 23 September – we learn that the Mussolini government has been officially reconstituted. Pavolini is its delegate in the capital, while the German General Maelzer, who resides at Hotel Excelsior, is the military commandant of Rome. Fearing that Nino's dispensation certificate is no longer valid, we place in the cellar a double-bottom wardrobe opening into a windowless cubby-hole that may one day prove invaluable.

THE RELATIVES FROM TRIESTE

We don't feel in much danger. Nor are we concerned for Mother's brother, Uncle Memmo, whose Jewish surname Liebman has been covered by the Aryan Marzi for enough years now to make it forgotten. Besides, he feels secure enough to become an anti-Fascist conspirator over the following months, carrying messages (I've never known from whom to whom) in the soles of his boots.

Those in real danger are our relatives in the North. We've heard nothing for weeks from our Ascoli cousins. Are they still in the countryside at Monteviale? The Liebmans from Trieste get in touch, sounding rather more worried and asking for help. They want to come to Rome, since they know it will be liberated first and that they can hide more easily there in the strange surroundings. Can we put them up? For a few weeks at most, since the Allies are already in the Salerno area.

They arrive – all of them. There is Aunt Lisa Liebman Barzilai, Grandfather's only surviving sister, as rosy, prickly and charming as ever; Aunt Ester Modiano Liebman, Grandfather's sister-in-law, as glum and petulant as ever; Uncle Vico Liebman, her son, a dilettante painter who has done nothing else in life, able to cream the profits from the paper mills that have provided a handsome living for all branches of his mother's family (the Modianos); and his wife, and cousin to boot, Aunt Anna Mentz. As for the other Triestini, all we know is that they escaped in time: Uncle Peppino Mentz, the son of Grandmother's sister Vittoria and a great friend of my father's (like him a hopeless aficionado of casinos and horse-racing), went away and took with him his cousin Italo Liebman (a young boy whose name reflects the family's obsession with Italic roots).

(Only after the war, when the first letters crossed the Atlantic, did we learn that Peppino and Italo had managed to reach the exotic port of Casablanca and to board a ship for America, where they found work in a 'chicken factory' – a form of industrial production unknown to us. They enclosed a photo of the factory-owner: she was a beautiful widow whom Peppino, a real ladies' man, ended up marrying. Neither he nor Italo would ever return to Italy.)

At the end of September, an entry in my diary records the arrival of my relatives from Trieste with a sense of excitement and adventure (though we are far from appreciating the risks), as well as a touch of irritation that we are being flooded with old people. For now we have living with us not only the aunts but also Grandmother and Fanny, Nino's very old mother from Sardinia. I no longer have a room of my own, and sleep on the sofa in the living-room.

For fear of a police search, the aunts are obliged every evening to repeat from memory the new Aryan particulars contained in the false documents we have procured for them. Aunt Lisa always makes a mistake when replying to the question: 'Whose daughter are you?' 'Lazzaro's', she says, instead of the correct answer: 'Giulio's'. We go over it again, calling her *scempia* [silly], as if in a theatre scene in the Trieste dialect.

The picture becomes clearer to us on 16 October, when the police raid the Ghetto.* I have never seen the Ghetto with my own eyes; indeed, I did not even know that such a thing existed. I know Jewish people, of course. But mine live elsewhere, mostly in the Parioli or Prati neighbourhood. I hear of the raid from the Tedeschi family, who live on Via Po: the Nazis showed up at dawn and Tedeschi, a lawyer, understood at once. He sacrificed himself by going to open the door, so that his wife and two children (my friends) would have time to escape by the servants' exit. They would never see him again.

News also reaches us of a Jewish acquaintance from Trieste: the lawyer Monteldi. He was arrested on the night of 15–16 October, in an inn on Via Vittoria where he thought he was safe.

Many non-Jews are also in hiding: young men who have failed to report for the call-up, which now starts from the year 1924 and

---

* On 16 October 1943, 1,024 Jews living in the Rome ghetto were rounded up and deported to Auschwitz.

ends with 1910. A lot of the ones I know are in a monastery; others, children of the 'black' papal bourgeoisie,* have enlisted in the Palatine Guard, the neutral army of the Vatican state. Still others, again through family connections, are serving in the Pattuglie Antincendio Italiane, a paramilitary force charged with patrolling the city in the event of air raids.

I don't like all this concealment. I don't know of any at all who, without actually fighting, do something to help the anti-Fascists – with the exception of the unlikely messages that Uncle Memmo carries in the soles of his shoes. I have no information about the Resistance, because my local area and milieu are not resisting and seem unaware that others are doing so elsewhere.

Those who are called 'the Allies' – and who are supposed to be the allies of us Italians – bomb too much for us to think of them as friends. 'The English', I write in my diary, with a certain irony, 'are advancing very calmly, but from the far end of Italy. And already they want to annex Sicily. The French accuse General Heisenhauer [*sic* – I couldn't have seen the name written anywhere] of betraying them, while he says that the traitors are the Fascists, and they call Badoglio "the betrayer of Italy" and speak of the Armistice as a "dirty deal". Therefore', I write disconsolately, 'we no longer know to whom we can turn to save the Fatherland' (still written then with a capital 'P' for *Patria*).

I still have esteem for Badoglio, however: his main defect is that he is an old man and did not know how to organize things. The king, on the other hand, is a 'cretin', and Mussolini a 'madman'. In

---

* A term used to describe those who sided with Pius X in 1870, when King Victor Emmanuel seized Rome and put an end to the independence of the Papal States.

support of this judgement, I refer to rumours that he suffers from progressive paralysis of the mind. But I also write of what is happening at Il Tasso, where I return to the fourth year of secondary school when classes finally resume.

Many of my schoolmates – those who have already finished or will soon be finishing school – have enlisted in the Decima MAS, the special marine corps. Why have they done this? I ask. They must know they will be dying for a cause that is already lost. And I add: 'Everyone despises them, calling them hoodlums and lily-livered.' This does not seem to me the right description, since (with reference to those joining the Palatine Guard) they rather display courage. If anything, I sympathize with them: 'They were Fascists like everyone and already felt themselves to be soldiers when they were fourteen, because they were taught in the GIL how to hold a rifle. On 26 July they saw their ideal collapse, and later, when the fog of "We shall conquer!" lifted, they saw the wretchedness of the regime. What else should they do now? They are enlisting out of a sense of dignity, not because they believe in victory. They are not arrogant, only melancholic.' In short, my ideas are different from theirs, but I do not despise them. I shake hands with Mario B., the unlucky lover of my friend L., who plays the hero's card and comes in uniform to say hello before leaving for the front. And I feel sure that, if an organization existed that fired at everyone, they would be the first to join it. What interests me are the endowments of courage and moral sense, not the problem or the conflict itself, nor who is right and who is wrong, or what would happen if the Decima MAS guys were to be victorious. Politics is not what matters when you are fourteen; you are looking for a moral compass, for guiding principles – the rest comes much later.

My agony is that is I do not have ideals. 'Which should we follow', I ask myself, 'the Communists or the Partito d'Azione,* who shoot at night in the street at a lone German or policeman on his way home, with the only result that the curfew starts an hour earlier? Or those who go off to the Abruzzo maquis and open fire on anyone who comes across them?' 'That's fine, perfectly fine, for now', I conclude, 'but can it last until the other friends arrive? And is it really the English that these so-called partisans are awaiting – perhaps then to enlist under the banners of the former enemy or Badoglio's men? Why should we now respect Badoglio? Or should we perhaps be for the king? For whom, then? What the devil is Italy?' In my anguish, I wonder what I would do if I were a man and a little more than fourteen.

I don't know what to answer, and the fact that I do not have to choose because I am female and adolescent makes me even more desperate.

Most seriously, I am convinced – because this is all I see around me – that large numbers are joining the Fascist 'M' Troops or Decima MAS: 'nearly all the boys I know in Rome', I write. And I report that they are running away from home to do it, for fear of being held back by parents who, for their part, seek to avoid the packs of Germans ordering office workers to move to the North. I myself hold these parents in contempt, 'because they profited from Fascism but disowned it as soon as it fell'.

'So, should we all be Fascists?' Fortunately I do not reach that conclusion. I recognize that those who were anti-Fascist previously – and I number myself among them – have a right to be so today.

---

* Radical anti-Fascist Republican party that existed between 1942 and 1947. *L'Italia Libera* was its official newspaper.

It is more difficult to take sides when I hear that the Negus, from his place of asylum in Switzerland, has called for Badoglio to be arrested for crimes committed in Ethiopia. The British refuse to accept this, while the Fascists are even more embarrassed. Remembering the things written about Abyssinia on my classroom walls at primary school, as well as the sentences about the 'little black face' that our teacher made us compile,* I understand less and less about all this.

The situation at home naturally influences my political shifts. First there is my irritation over my Jewish relatives: I completely underestimate the risks they face (we know nothing about the camps, of course) and see only a petty desire to save themselves and their legacy without bothering about the rest of the world. The fact that they are persecuted and threatened with deportation simply because they are non-Aryan does not seem to me sufficient.

Also I am fed up with all these old women who in the evening – since the curfew means I have to stay home – force me to make up a bridge foursome. What with Grandmother, Aunt Lisa and Aunt Ester, who see badly and don't remember which cards they have in their hand – I can't take any more! And then there is the daily recital of the particulars in their identity papers, the confusion between Giulio and Lazzaro, and so on.

The atmosphere is more cheerful on the floor below ours, where the 'young people' live: Mother and Nino, Uncle Vico and Aunt Anna.

Uncle Vico is witty but also very spoilt. He remained the only child after his elder brother, Roberto, was forced to join the Austrian

---

* An allusion to the Fascist song 'Faccetta Nera', which promised the Ethiopian population that Italy would soon be bringing the benefits of its civilization.

army in the First World War and was killed by an Italian bullet. I have never known the political sympathies of his father, the brother of Grandfather Liebman, but at the age of seventeen (almost half a century earlier) he ran away from home and Trieste with his great friend Guglielmo Oberdan to avoid serving in the Austro-Hungarian army. At heart he probably shared the ideas of his other brothers, who, like the educated middle classes of Trieste in general, were all Italophiles. That friendly (but officially hostile) fire which killed his favourite son must have been a particularly hard blow for him.

This additional pain was not felt by Aunt Ester, his rich wife, for whom Italy was of little consequence. She was a Modiano, and the Modianos were Sephardi, not Ashkenazi like the Liebmans. They came from Salonica, where the beautiful markets that bear their name have been restored after a number of fires. Like so many other Sephardi Jewish merchants, they went to Trieste in the 1600s when it was declared a free port and became a convenient place from which to do business.

I read about these things in the letters that Uncle Nino Pontini, the only survivor of the Spanish Cusin branch of my family, scrupulously preserved until his death. Their daughter Dircea – whose yellowed photograph I still have on my dressing-table, although she lived almost a century before me – was given in marriage to the father of Grandfather Adolfo Liebman.

The Cusins always intrigued me, because Uncle Pontini's collection of letters contained some from one of the cousins twice removed in Vienna, where he had been sent to study. They were dated 1848 and bore the extraordinary marks of that '68 of old. The cousin had sent them to his sister in Trieste, asking her to keep them hidden from his father since he would be very angry to find out about his involvement in politics. They told of the revolutionary movements that were shaking the Imperial capital, while his sister – judging by his replies – sent excited news of what was said to be happening in Budapest and Trieste itself: the Italian tricolour unfurled at a special re-enactment of the Challenge of Barletta in the Teatro Grande;* the entry of the king of Sardinia's fleet, under Admiral Albini, into the harbour of Trieste, together with Venetian and Neapolitan naval forces; the raising of the Italian flag on every treetop. She also wrote to him about the deployment of Austrian heavy artillery at the Cathedral of San Giusto, the Lazzaretto Vecchio and the San Carlo Quay, to crush any stirrings of independence.

To be frank, it was not understood too well why they had been so pro-Italian. The evidence pointed to an unwillingness to bear the rigidity of Habsburg conservatism – a student rebellion against authority more than anything else.

The older generation of Cusins were very conservative, however, as one can tell from the life-stories they gradually left behind. (It is a Jewish tradition that people on their death bed write down not only which possessions they wish to bequeath to whom but also a critical balance sheet of their life.) Uncle Beniamino, hit by the crisis of the Twenties (the 1820s), even asked his future widow to forgive him for the collapse of the insurance company where he had been head, the Assicurazioni Generali di Sicurtà. It was a disaster from which the family would never completely recover, and those who came after had to branch out from commerce or finance into the less lucrative careers of doctor or lawyer. All the same, they seem to have been left enough to continue inserting the ritual phrases in

---

* Challenge of Barletta: a famous tournament fought in 1503 in Southern Italy between thirteen Italians and thirteen French knights, following an incident when one of the latter, under the influence of drink, accused the Italians of cowardice.

their will: 'I leave 20 florins to help with the dowry of a marriageable and impecunious young lady of our religion, and 5 florins to the Christian maid currently in service.'

In the new generation, my *triestini* seemed much less conformist: completely free to fall in and out of love, but also to stay with a lover without leaving their spouse. They travelled and had fun: photos of chic holiday resorts, tennis courts, horse races, cruises, women with silk 'palace pyjamas' of the kind that would be fashionable again half a century later, men in straw hats. My mother's letters and stories described to me the life of that pleasure-seeking Central Europe of the Twenties and Thirties, which I had had time to catch a whiff of only at the Venice Lido. It certainly bore no traces of Jewish religiosity: only the attribute 'goy', spoken with a turned-up nose about anyone not fortunate enough to be a Jew.

Mother, very 'goy' at heart, had been more a spectator than a player in that world. She and her sister Vittorina had trailed around as poor subaltern nieces, daughters of a crazy brother (my grandfather Adolfo) missing for decades, forced to accompany their rich aunts to Vichy or Karlsbad or Monte Carlo – half ladies in waiting, half potential matches on display for any suitors who might show up. It was a hateful condition for young Roman women like them, whose secular, intellectual background was relatively free of prejudices, though still subject to economic constraints.

Mother had always been bored stiff with her aunts, partly because they had never stopped whispering criticism about the condition in which their inconsiderate brother Adolfo had left his family.

They were not so in the wrong, the poor things. They too had been through difficult moments, but they had known how to keep a clear head and secure their privileged status. Though very good-looking, Aunt Vittoria and Aunt Lisa could not offer much of a dowry: the Liebmans were comfortably off, not wealthy. They both married more than once, gaining for themselves a more than serene old age – at least until the race laws descended on the country, in a sudden turn of events that should have been expected more widely than it was. After all, some signs from Nazi Germany must have got through, and the Rome–Berlin Axis should have raised some fears and given a boost to anti-Fascism.

But it did not raise any: and it made them neither Fascist nor anti-Fascist, only happy-go-lucky. At most they felt a little irritated with Uncle Guido Liebman, a cousin of theirs who became an enthusiastic member of the militias after Mussolini's March on Rome. They thought his fez especially unseemly, and I too had a chance to laugh at it when I saw him wearing it in photos strewn around the house.

Aunt Vittoria, Grandfather's eldest sister, was a key figure in my life. Indeed, I would not have been born without her, since she was the one who arranged marriages. Mother's stunningly beautiful sister Vittorina was married off to the surly Venetian lawyer Renzo Ascoli, without being asked for her opinion in the matter. He was a good match – that was enough. Besides, she was happy to escape her aunts' clutches in this way.

My mother became engaged at Cortina d'Ampezzo – at the Hotel Bellevue, to be precise – in August 1925. Her suitor, Gino Castellina, had entered our circle because he was great friends with Peppino Mentz, the madcap son of Aunt Vittoria who ended up in that American chicken factory. Neither of them had a lira to their name, but they liked the good life and therefore had the appearance of being rich.

Mother too seemed rich, thanks to the life she had with her aunt. But she and Gino Castellina confessed the truth to each other as soon as they were allowed to be alone together. 'Look', Mother apparently told him, 'I don't even know if the blouse on my back is mine.' He laughed, it seems, and warned her that he too was penniless.

This pre-emptive confession on both sides created an attachment between them, making up for, I won't say love, but for what they lacked in common interests and culture. It proved so strong that, when her aunt realized her mistake and tried to call off the betrothal, the couple proudly insisted: no, now we're going to get married. (In the account Mother gave of her life in her nineties – which the publisher Pepe Laterza later printed for friends – she was more specific: 'I married Gino Castellina because I'd kissed him.')

In protest, Aunt Vittoria refused to attend the wedding. This proved a big hurdle years later at the annulment proceedings before the Sacra Rota, when an attempt was made to invoke the clause in the Code of Canon Law referring to unwillingness of one of the two parties. How could someone not even present at the ceremony have forced Mother to marry Gino Castellina? It was too difficult to enlighten the holy prelates at San Giovanni in Latero about the sometimes contradictory workings of the human soul.

All these events explain how it was that, although my parents realized by 1934 that they were not made for each other, relations between them remained excellent. Father regularly came to visit Grandmother, for whom he felt real devotion, and often stayed for lunch even after Mother had remarried. Many a time in that winter of 1943–44, an addition was made to the happy band of 'young' Liebmans living on the first floor of the Salis house.

Father's own home – or rather his lover's home, where he moved after the Hotel Minerva closed up because of the war – provided lodging for two other cousins of my mother's from Trieste: Uncle

Guido and Aunt Lina Liebman. Father was an old friend of Uncle Guido; when he was the referring doctor at the Hotel Excelsior, the two would suddenly head off in an ambulance with sirens wailing to the Capannelle race track, armed with a last-minute tip.

PADRE STEFANU

Father's visits – I record in my diary – now also have a practical purpose. Only he is really 'legal' and therefore in a position to move around without fear, obtaining food for the whole community. When nothing can be found even at the Tor di Nona black market, a long family summit decides to sacrifice Nino's magnificent Bianchi, the six-cylinder car with beige leather seats and interior bags, which consumes a litre of petrol every hundred metres and for that reason has remained in the garage since '36 (when the British imposed sanctions on Italy and the roads were forbidden to such vehicles).

There are tears in his eyes as a lucky mechanic takes away the long automobile to convert it into a pickup. It is with this recycled vehicle that Father then travels the countryside near Rome, defying constant strafing and road blocks in search of eggs, flour, butter, oil and chickens. He takes along an old friend: Padre Stefanu, the priest who celebrated Mother's marriage to Nino and eventually became my confidant/confessor. He belongs to the non-Orthodox Greek Rite, a rare order with a monastery near San Giovanni, and whether out of personal conviction or because of flexible rules he behaves in a rather more modern way than all the other priests I know.

He is tall and handsome, sporting a long, dark beard, and is a cultured and witty person. Mother found him in a confessional at the Church of San Bellarmino, when her Aryanization case was underway and the lawyer Le Pera had advised her to show her face in a parish. Apparently he helped clear the way for her 'mixed' marriage with the Aryan Nino to go ahead.

Mother was a little embarrassed. Although baptized in a church, she had not set foot in one for years except to attend my first communion and confirmation. But she plucked up courage and knelt down in the first confessional she found on entering the church on Piazza Ungheria. The priest behind the grille seemed nice enough, and so she told him the whole truth about why she was there. So it was that Padre Stefanu soon became a household friend and ended up officiating at her wedding.

That autumn, Padre Stefanu too needed to obtain food for the rest of the monastery. So the joint venture got underway: Nino put in the car, the cousins from Trieste the capital, Father – neither Jew nor deserter – his entrepreneurship, and Padre Stefanu a traffic pass issued by the Vatican. With Father acting as chauffeur, they had no trouble persuading any policeman to let them drive on. 'We're from the Greek monastery of San Giovanni in Laterano', they would say.

PARTISANS

On 20 October, I finally realize that the partisans are a real force and not just a few motley groups that have gone off into the maquis. But they are still 'bands' who commit injustices: in the Gorizia region, moreover, fighting with the Slovenes.

I read this in the Roman daily *Il Messagero*, our only source of information. Unlike many others, we are unable to listen to Radio London: we have too many Jews in hiding to take such risks, and the news broadcast by Colonel Stevens reaches us only at second hand, from friends in better standing with the law. Anyway, even

Radio London seems to make little mention of those partisans; it talks only of the Allied troops who keep advancing but never arrive.

I learn some more from Giorgio Tecce, speaking in a conspiratorial undertone as we queue up for water at the fountain on the corner of Via Mercati and Via Linneo. (Forty years later, he would go on to become rector of Rome's Sapienza university.) We live next door to each other and he also attends Il Tasso, but although we have often passed each other in the street he is older than me and we have not really become acquainted before. These are obviously special times: otherwise such a big boy would not have said a word to a little girl like me. I still wear knee socks and, though fourteen by now, I am as pretty as a rake. I haven't even started my periods, but I keep this a secret because I'd no longer carry any weight with my friends if they knew.

To tell the truth, my friends are few and far between: many have dropped out of sight because the war has led them to move elsewhere, forced them into hiding or – in most cases – taken them away. Even the brother of my bosom friend Annalena has enlisted in the Decima MAS. He was the most fascinating and cultured of the boys I used to know, and I am much affected by his departure. (Having narrowly escaped during the events of 1944–45, Gianfranco Baruchello would become a highly thought-of protagonist in all the cultural avant-gardes and go on to join one of the most extreme New Left groups: Potere Operaio.)

IL TASSO

School reopens on 9 November. After the interval in Verona, here I am back at Il Tasso, in the same austere building where I attended my first two secondary classes. Paolo the caretaker is still there; so too is headmaster Amante, also known as Saracca for his lanky figure.* Il Duce once singled him out for praise because he had shown exemplary courage in sending his son Romano off to fight, and this recognition made him still more Fascist than before. But it did not stop him removing the bust of Bruno Mussolini on 26 July, immediately after his father's arrest, from the entrance hall where it had been placed two years earlier following his death in the war. (Fortunately for Amante, he thought better of this before it was too late, so that the statue was back in place when we returned in the autumn.)

We no longer have the 'terrible' Signora Cutzer as our maths teacher; nor is Paola Della Pergola there as *professoressa*. Some students are also missing. 'They've gone away', we are told. Because they're Jewish, it is said *sotto voce*.

Someone tells me that a few anti-Fascists have been leaving leaflets around. There aren't any in my class, 4D: if there were I'd have noticed. I prick up my ears, but no luck.

(I came across them only after the Liberation – or, to be more precise, I realized only then who they were and what they had been doing. They were Citto Maselli, Roberto Inverardi, Sandro Curzi, the Savioli and Pirandello brothers, and Lietta Tornabuoni. Though still very young, they were part of some Communist underground organization linked to the PCI and active in Rome. That year they saw school as a training ground for political action; little girls like us weren't even worth recruiting.)

One day I too realize that something dramatic has happened, since the teachers are whispering among themselves and there is general confusion on the storey with the classrooms. Two former

---

* *Saracca* or *salacca*, an Italian word for sardine, is also a colloquial expression for a very skinny person.

pupils, Luigi Pintor and Alfredo Reichlin (my future husband), burst into the headmaster's office, guns in hand, and warn him not to interfere in the student strike called over the killing of Massimo Gizzio by Fascists in front of the Liceo Dante Alighieri, in the Prati district.

We do not manage to find out the number and identity of the strikers, or what has actually been going on. There are no anti-Fascists among my classmates: we are all very ignorant, we still wear black aprons like children, and our greatest transgression, on the way home, is to stop at the Fassi ice cream store on the Corso d'Italia.

But even that pleasure does not last long, because 'Gigetto', the English airman (who knows how he acquired that affectionate diminutive?), shows up punctually at midday over the south of the city and directs some machine-gun fire at the Castelli Romani. The time of our departure is therefore brought forward to 11:45, so that we can get home in time. But the air raid alarm always catches us at the tram stop on Piazza Fiume, and no one bothers about it. In any case, isn't Rome an 'open city'?

MUSHROOMS

Our greatest scare during the months of German occupation was on account of mushrooms. Mother found some for sale on a street corner and happily brought them home. It was a big event to have such things to feast on.

One evening, grandparents, aunts, cousins and I started to vomit one after another. We had no milk, the traditional antidote – only some of the condensed stuff, too little of it and very sweet, and Aunt Ester, who was feeling the worst, could not drink any because of her diabetes. We rang Uncle Guido Liebman and asked for his advice as a doctor. There were two dangers: either we could die of poisoning or we might be arrested in hospital for possession of false papers. Uncle Guido, sure that we were otherwise bound for the hereafter, recommended the second option: to call the emergency services straight away.

We took his advice with some trepidation. After a couple of tense hours, during which the ambulance never dreamed of coming to help, we were all feeling better and went to sleep. At daybreak, however, a prolonged ringing of the bell woke us up. We immediately thought: the Germans. Nino rushed down to the cellar, through the wardrobe with a false bottom. Again and again we fretfully reminded Aunt Lisa that she was the daughter of Giulio, not Lazzaro, and did our best to calm Aunt Ester. Mother peeped through the gate, but then, while we all held our breath, she turned and gave a loud laugh. It was the ambulance, five hours late; we could all have been dead but were fortunately well on the mend.

A few weeks later we had a similar scare, around seven in the morning. This time there really were two German officers at the gate, looking into the garden and running their eyes up and down the windows. Nino made another dash for the cupboard and the aunts were alerted again, while Mother, all straight with the law, went down and tried to gain some time. Finally, everything took a farcical turn. The soldiers were a couple of romantics: they had come to photograph the house where their German fiancées lived. The girls, employees at the German embassy, had rented the top floor while we were in Verona and were due to return home on 8 September. The boys were leaving for the front and wanted a reminder of the blissful times they had spent there (as they put it with a bitter sadness in their voice).

DECEMBER 1943: CHRISTMAS

General Maelzer, the military commandant of Rome, has eased the curfew as a Christmas present: it will begin at 9 p.m. instead of 7 p.m. But the atmosphere in the city doesn't make us feel like wandering around, so we don't know what to do with ourselves during the extra two hours. At home we are still living in make-shift isolation, with no news and on tenterhooks. We wonder what has become of the Ascoli. When we manage to get through to the telephone exchange, they tell us there is no answer at Monteviale.

Matches and salt are rationed. But the Orchestra of Santa Cecilia has announced its concert season, a little later than usual. The war has reached the Volturno valley and the islands of the *Odyssey*.

29 JANUARY 1944: THE ANZIO LANDING

On 29 January I refer to the landing a few days earlier at Anzio. We can hear artillery fire, and it is said that the Abbey of Monte Cassino has been destroyed. Allied pilots are razing Italy to the ground. I feel angry about the hunger, destitution and disease facing the people. 'The British are dreadful,' I write. Moroccans and Poles are also pushing up from the South. 'To free ourselves of one for-eigner, we have ended up having armies from half the world. The Italians have made the same mistakes over the centuries. We are a deluded people, doomed to serve others because we are no good at commanding. Now our Fatherland – I mean the homeland of true Italians, not of the Fascists, but also not of the Communists who debase themselves in Bolshevism – is on the point of being lost: we no longer have any honour.'

My pessimism was at its height, my political thinking no more than an adaptation of school reading to the new context. Grown-ups make me laugh, I write, when they say that life is worth living and ridicule the disgust we feel for the human race. Looking back today, I wonder how we tried to think when we knew so little. Unlike Socrates, we were not even aware that we knew nothing.

8 MARCH 1944

Gigetto is no longer an affable pilot who flies over the suburbs, not daring to bomb the 'open city'. The B-17s and Wellingtons are now striking savage blows, in broad daylight. Their main target is Garbatella, a district I think is on the outer fringes of Rome but is really almost in the centre, near the Ostiense freight yard. Nor do I know much about the so-called 'quickie suburbs' of Il Trullo, Tiburtino III, Pietralata, Val Melaina, Tor Marancia and Quarticciolo, hastily erected for those made homeless by Mussolini's gutting of Borgo Vecchio and Borgo Nuovo and of the area between the Colosseum and the Capitoline Hill. Perhaps, when they are bombed, the newspapers do not even report it.

In the case of Garbatella, though, I read the news and record with horror and incredulity the brief item in *Il Messagero*: 'The terror from the sky rained down on densely populated Garbatella. A child of two, Andreina Proietti, was pulled from the rubble of the Albergo dei Poveri' (which, I learn, is the name for some housing set aside for the homeless). 'Also: churches, workers' housing, religious institutions and crèches have been hit and destroyed in the Ostiense, Testaccio and Portuense districts.' 'Holes the size of craters seem to have appeared on Via Adolfo Hitler [today's Via Marco Polo]', I write, and 'at home we sneer because they seem to have appeared on the very body of the one who gave his name to the street.' But although I am told that bombing brings the end of the war closer, I continue to ask myself what is the purpose of the killing; and as I can't find a convincing answer, my contempt for the British keeps growing.

BIANCHINA

The afternoons are very short. There is just time to go to a cinema, where the performances now begin at three. I see *Le Bonheur*, with Charles Boyer and Michel Simon, and like it a lot. Then it's straight back home: the curfew descends at seven, but the trams stop running at six and it's not possible to travel by bike after five. So we only see people close by; it's as if everyone else is living in a different city.

I find a new friend: she lives a few houses beyond the end of my street. The aunts from Trieste, who used to know her grandmother, take me there. Bianchina Riccio is only thirteen but has the right to wear long stockings. I can't take my eyes off her hairdo, and she keeps looking at my knee-length socks; I go to Il Tasso, while she attends the school run by the Sisters of the Sacred Heart of Jesus. But the curfew does not allow us to be too picky. After a few weeks we are close friends, sometimes sleeping over at each other's houses.

I am not at her place on the night when the Germans burst in. They find an old grandmother, a mother (Milaide) and two children: Bianchina and her younger sister, Nicoletta. Their father was head of the Banca d'Italia in Addis Ababa when the British took him prisoner there at the beginning of the war.

Agitated and terrified, Bianchina comes round the next morning and tells us what happened. There was an officer (the notorious Erich Priebke, we later found out) and a number of soldiers, who took her mother off to the SS prison in Via Tasso. We know it is an infernal place, but not much else.

It is understood that her grandmother knows more, but she doesn't say much because she's afraid that, what with all the Jews hidden in our house, she might compromise us and especially them.

(When I think back today it seems strange that, although the trauma of German occupation touched so closely on my life, it did not shake me as much as it should have.)

After Milaide is taken away, I know about the arrests and the direct German involvement in them. But it's still not clear to me why they took Milaide or what they intended to do with her. I have learned of the round-ups of people for forced labour, either here or in Germany, because decrees are published in the press and everyone is afraid to move around, especially by tram (where they suddenly make everyone get off and check their papers, then take off the ones who seem sufficiently able-bodied). My people therefore stay shut up indoors; only Mother ever goes out, plus me on my way to and from school. And Father with Padre Stefanu.

I am also dimly aware that they are taking Jews away. But Milaide is neither male nor Jewish. Why was she snatched from her home in the middle of the night? As far as I know, she lives next door to some aristocrats and is the sister of an admiral in the Navy (the branch of the armed forces most loyal to the monarchy). So, she's certainly not the type to have anything to do with the Resistance, which, on the rare occasions when it's mentioned in the papers, is described as a collection of bandits.

(Only after the liberation of Rome would I discover more about the fate of my friend Bianchina's mother: that she was taken to the SS prison in Via Tasso; that she was locked up in a cell next to Montezemolo, the king's aide-de-camp, who had fled from the War Ministry when the Germans liquidated the last remnants of an Italian authority; that she heard the groans of people returning from the torture chambers; that through the walls she could hear the bustling of prison wardens and the order given in German for a group to be taken away and shot at the Fosse Ardeatine.* I understood nothing at the time, even after Milaide was released, but Rome was still occupied then and it would have been too dangerous to breathe a word – both for her and for the monarchist resistance group she had managed to put together.)

In ten months of Nazi occupation, then, the only Resistance with which I had any actual contact was the one mounted by the Royal Italian Navy, which Bianchina's mother secretly assisted.

My diary records Milaide's return from Via Tasso on 16 April. 'It was four in the afternoon. I was going up Via Mercati towards Via Aldovrandi when I saw a woman limping along in the other direction, dragging a large shopping bag behind her. At first I didn't realize who it was. Then my heart skipped a beat: it's Milaide! I didn't know whether I should run up to her or race back to tell Bianchina, who lived a few houses away. I awkwardly did both at the same time, moving up and down the street, until Bianchina and Nicoletta finally arrived. Her grandmother, too shaken up, stayed at the window.

'She'd been released, but she was very thin, looked pale and had a look in her eyes that I'd never seen before. Emotions were running very high: tears, kisses, everyone standing around, soon joined by my mother. But she didn't want to talk.'

In fact, even afterwards when the danger was over, I only heard her say a few words about the dramatic experience – partly because of her natural reserve, but perhaps also because the memory of it was too horrific.

---

* On 24 March 1944, German troops carried out a notorious mass execution at the Ardeantine caves in Rome, in reprisal for a partisan attack.

War

18 MARCH 1944: GRANDFATHER

Gigetto has flown across the barrier into the 'open city'. Rather than simply shoot from on high over the Castelli and the outer fringes of Rome, he has pressed on to Piazza Galeno and the Verano cemetery. Bombs are said to have fallen on tombs in the southern side, behind the wall separating it from the Portonaccio district. It is the location of our grave, the Liebman one, which holds the body of Mother's other sister, Aunt Marialena, and the ashes of Grandfather Adolfo (who was cremated at his own wish).

My aunt matters to me less. Ever since I first heard her name, it has been preceded by the adjective *povera*: poor Aunt Marialena, stricken from birth with a heart ailment that eventually killed her at such a young age. I had no chance to get to know her; all I have left of her are some faded photographs that show her with a sad sweet smile.

But Grandfather is important: he died only in 1935, when I was already nearly six, so there are many pictures of us together.

I worshipped him, as he did me, even though the dialogue between us consisted only of smiles and caresses. We also exchanged drawings on odd pieces of paper. They always showed signs of a shaky hand: mine because I was still a novice, his because he was at the end of a painting career which, though never exercised in public, had made him famous in circles of friends, above all as a caricaturist. After returning from a ten-year absence abroad, he came down with a terrible disease which, among other things, robbed him of the power of speech. It was 1923 and he was already feeling bad when he landed in Naples and had difficulty recognizing his younger daughter, my mother; she had been a child when he left and now she was almost twenty.

After much wandering through Latin America, he started a small transport business – 'Consignments from and to Bolivia' – up in

La Quiaca, a Bolivian mining region three thousand metres above sea level. But it was a miserable failure, and this, together with the climate and melancholia, gradually wore him down. In the many letters he sent home, which I found in various boxes, he begged his son Guglielmo not to join him there (as he would have liked), saying that only an old man could bear to live in such a place without being overwhelmed with nostalgia for trees, fields and water – in short, for life itself. 'Here', he wrote, 'it's not like in Buenos Aires; the only society consists of Turks, Spaniards and Bolivians – all of them people who would fit well in the lower depths of our cities.' When health complaints forced him to move down to the valley, in Argentina, he continued to worry about Italy. The war had not been over for long and the political climate was uncertain. The hostility of the local press made him feel frustrated: 'the news reports about Italy', he wrote, 'describe the country in criminal colours'. The only bright spot was the arrival of a certain *Onorevole** Orlando, who 'turned out to be a highly likeable figure, able to win over everyone, Italian and Argentinean, and to convey an unflagging breath of patriotism'.

His never-ending letters, written in a small flawless hand, list and criticize his own shortcomings: 'Too much enthusiasm for any venture, without weighing the obstacles and difficulties that are often too great for my powers; inordinate trust and credence in everyone; exaggerated and ridiculous compassion for people suffering through no fault of mine.'

Although everything went badly for him, he kept postponing his return to Europe – despite the fact that, at the end of the war, his

---

* *Onorevole* [Honourable]: the title used in Italy for members of parliament.

dream that Trieste would become Italian had finally been achieved. He was ashamed to appear penniless before his wife and children. 'I am in the twilight of my life', he wrote to Grandmother before he came back, 'and I have still not managed to put aside the wherewithal to keep you when you are left alone.'

Together with the letters, I discover an invaluable diary that Grandmother kept at the time – a little book of bound parchment. Inside, the pages are thickly covered with the right-sloping script commonly used in the nineteenth century, in the middle of which (1863) she had been born into a family of sanctimonious landowners in Tarquinia.

Grandmother's diary begins thirty years later, rather a long way from her native Maremma, in San Salvador de Jujuy, the capital of Salta province far up in the borderland straddling Chile, Bolivia and Argentina; it is the back of beyond today, so we can imagine what it was like then. She tells of her existence as a young wife transplanted from Rome to a godforsaken *finca* among the sugar-cane and tobacco plantations, where Grandfather has gone to exercise the not so congenial duties of estate manager, to which he adds the honorary function of consul of the Kingdom of Italy. The diary is full of stories of young Italians who, having gone there in search of work, are helped to escape the clutches of grasping landowners. But there are also continual references to what is happening in her distant, and still sadly missed, homeland. Above all, she feels nostalgia for the Christmases of her childhood, with all the house guests and games of tombola and ring-shaped cakes; it was so cold in the halls of the Palazzo della Commenda in Tarquinia (the home of the Marzi family before they became scattered), whereas in Jujuy, where she lives now, the heat is a killer and there is no question of lighting a fire.

But apart from personal nostalgia, there is actual pain over the tragedy 'of our brother Italians subject to the barbarian Menelik'* and, later, over the mourning 'inflicted on us when our beloved King Umberto was ignobly assassinated by a human wild beast'.[†] The news, arriving by telegraph from across the ocean, becomes interwoven with the everyday reality of Jujuy: flight on horseback at the approach of bandits; the chewing of coca and, to her extreme disgust, its passing from mouth to mouth; the disaster of the tilbury carriage, a present from Grandfather, which was destroyed by a mad runaway horse. Above all, she tells of the healthy growth of her first child, born in Jujuy and baptised Guglielmo, but also known as Memmo, in honour of Oberdan.[‡]

Oberdan (with a Slovene surname) and Grandfather (with an Austrian one) felt themselves to be Italian because the Empire of Franz Joseph was a symbol of despotism. It may also be that for Grandfather, as for other Triestine Jewish intellectuals, part of his hatred had to do with the Imperial climate of anti-Semitism and the attractiveness of the new Kingdom of Italy, where, following the break with the Vatican, many Jews occupied key public positions.

The two men, who had first got to know each other at the Gymnasium in Trieste, joined the pro-Italian *Martello* [Hammer]

---

* Italian colonists began to settle in Ethiopia in the last quarter of the nineteenth century, and a small community remained there under the rule of Menelik II after Italy was defeated at the Battle of Adwa (1896).

† Umberto I, king of Italy from 1878 on, was assassinated in July 1900 by the anarchist Gaetano Bresci, who declared that his purpose had been to avenge the massacre of Milanese workers two years earlier.

‡ Guglielmo Oberdan (born Wilhelm Oberdank, 1858–82): a much-celebrated Italian irredentist born in Trieste. He was executed after a failed attempt to assassinate Emperor Franz Joseph of Austria.

group – a name intended to suggest that it was necessary to keep hammering away at the subject of the city's Italian identity.

In 1878, when 'the Austrian eagle stretched its talons towards Bosnia and Herzegovina and called upon the new levy of army conscripts to occupy those lands and crush their rebellious mountain peoples', Oberdan and Grandfather decided to desert, and got a fishing boat to put them ashore secretly near Ravenna. Still very young, they agreed between themselves to decide with other conspirators by a throw of the dice who should go off and assassinate Franz Joseph. The man to whom it fell took fright, and so Oberdan put himself forward instead; we know how that would end up.

Grandmother told me a thousand times of the heroic deeds of those youthful *triestini*. But it was only many years later that Alfred Alexander's *The Hanging of Wilhelm Oberdank* (which Bianchina found on a street stall in London and gave to me as a present) revealed the details of their thoughtless action.

The book, which contains many of Grandfather's letters, mentions that Adolfo Liebman and Oberdan, together with a delegation of exiles from Trento and Trieste, met Garibaldi in 1879 at Rome's Termini station. But it also says that the story found in every Italian textbook, according to which Garibaldi planted a kiss on the forehead of the famous irredentist, was a pure invention of Adolfo Liebman's. On the basis that he had personally witnessed the occasion, he wrote forty-five years later: 'Oberdank entreated him on his knees to help Trieste. Garibaldi promised aid and Oberdank, filled with emotion, kissed his hand. Thereupon Garibaldi kissed Oberdank on the forehead and said, "This kiss is for you and your comrades."'*

---

* Alfred Alexander, *The Hanging of Wilhelm Oberdank* (London: London Magazine Editions, 1977), p. 202.

It was in Rome, during the conspiracy years, that Grandfather met my grandmother Maria, a foundling barely twenty year old; it was love at first sight. The only problem was that, after a period at a Benedictine convent (where nuns in the 1870s used to hide children under the bed for fear of what Garibaldi might do to them), she and her six brothers had been entrusted to the uncles who were deans, who, as was usually the case in families of landowners, lived at home rather than in cloisters. For them it was unimaginable that she should marry a Jew.

In despair, Grandfather then left for Argentina. But Grandmother refused to marry anyone else and, meeting a friend of Grandfather's eight years later, asked him: 'Where is Adolfo now?' The answer: 'He's in Buenos Aires and thinks of you all the time.' So she wrote to him and he wired back: 'Come.' What she had not dared to do at the age of twenty, she found the courage for now. With her brother's help she went to Genoa and boarded a ship, her only guarantee being that telegraphic message.

On the ship, she saw a number of drawings fixed to the wall of the room where she ate her meals during the long crossing. The captain invited her to his table, and she asked him who had done them. 'A great friend of mine: Adolfo Liebman.' To which Maria Marzi replied: 'The very man I'm going to marry.' And so it was that, when they arrived at Boca, the port of Buenos Aires, the captain exercised his right to perform the marriage ceremony on board, without publishing the bans that might have proved a major embarrassment for Grandmother.

There was laughter in her eyes when she recounted to me this decisive chapter of her life. It was truly a great love, which lasted a lifetime. She died at the age of ninety-six, having joined the Italian Communist Party 'from a sense of dignity', as she put it.

When I went to Buenos Aires for the first time, I walked the streets looking for some family traces and came close to tears as I thought of my grandmother's life in that distant land. She could rely on no supports in the face of so many hardships: not always blows of fate but sometimes the result of Grandfather's follies, such as the construction of an Italian theatre that was later burned down. In 1904 he finally pressed her to return, with three children and a fourth, my mother, on the way.

It was a stormy departure, Grandmother said. After their luggage had been loaded, Grandfather persuaded the family to take a coach for a ride around the city – a last farewell to Argentina. So, by the time they returned to the port, the ship had already pulled away from its moorings and they had to catch it up by taking a fast boat to Rosario.

Grandfather remained her 'great love' even when another venture, a graphic arts business on the slopes of Villa Borghese, went bankrupt after his return to Italy and had to be sold off to its manager, Palombi (still active today). Once more he set sail for Argentina, equipped with a recently invented magic lantern, to give lectures about the Moon. He had an abundance of hackneyed material on the subject, which he embroidered and illustrated.

The family was supposed to join him there, but the outbreak of war put an end to such plans. In fact, they had to leave their temporary lodgings in Trieste with great haste, since they were Italians and therefore counted as enemies.

They then spent nearly ten years in Rome and were happy there. At home I still have many pictures or written reminders of that period, when the Liebman works was a meeting place for the progressive and bohemian intellectuals who went to the Pontine Fields southeast of Rome to spread literacy among the peasantry.

(Recently, during restoration work on a stained patch of one of Duilio Cambellotti's paintings, I found a moving dedication: 'To Comrade Adolfo Liebman.' They were among the first socialist intellectuals.)

So Grandfather, a bit of a hero, a bit of a hippy, was ready to give up everything for love or patriotism. How could he not have been a mythical figure for me? And in late 1944, ten years after the morning on which Mother told me that 'Grandad' had flown up to the sky, how could I not feel that the bombs which had perhaps scattered his ashes were raining down on me too? That air raid on Verano cemetery (which did not actually destroy the Liebman grave) was for me the most serious injury of the war – even though it was a dead not a living person who came under attack.

AUNT VITTORINA

The really painful moment of the war – the kind of direct, personal pain that sears your flesh and stifles your breathing – came for me on 29 April 1944. I was in my room when I heard screaming next door: it was from Grandmother, who was alone at the time. A shout: 'No, no, it isn't true … It can't be true!' The first reaction to a death that strikes someone without rhyme or reason is simple incredulity, a refusal to take it in. The war had carried off Aunt Vittorina, the mother of my twin cousin Luciano and Paoletta, the sweet, beautiful wife of Uncle Renzo Ascoli, whose Jewish blood had combined with our mixed ancestry to make the whole family subject to persecution under the Fascist laws.

As it happened, we received some post that morning – an unusual event during those months, although we had had no news of our relatives and always waited apprehensively for something to arrive. The Ascoli, particularly close to us, had shown no sign of life since their telephone in Monteviale (where they remained after the events of 8 September) had stopped answering.

There was a letter that day, 29 April. Written a long time before by friends who had taken refuge in Lugano, it had completed a mind-boggling journey to Rome via Portugal from Switzerland – both neutral countries. They took on the painful task of informing us. And upon opening that envelope, so invested with hopes, Grandmother learned that Vittoria, her third child born in Buenos Aires, had crashed onto the rocks on the north side of the Bernina glacier (the one that makes its way down from the Valtelline to Lake Lugano). It happened one night in early December, as people-smugglers were trying to cross the frontier along high mountain paths, not using torches so as not to alert the Fascist patrols. Aunt Vittorina took a false step and was swallowed up by the gorge, with her children behind her and her husband a little way in front.

They searched for her all night on the Swiss side, for which they had been heading. But all they found of her were bits and pieces, which have now been placed together in the small cemetery at Campolongo. Aunt Vittorina was forty-three, Luciano fourteen, Paoletta twenty.

The last time we had heard from them was on 6 October; I still have their yellowed postcard from Monteviale, with a stamp bearing the image of King Victor Emmanuel III. Luciano says he feels sorry for me because 'life must be hard in Rome', whereas 'here everything is very calm and we are well, thank God'. The only problem: *Lumi*, the comic we had been exchanging with friends in Venice, has had to cease publication; the post functions so badly. But Luciano is happy: 'Have you heard the news?' he writes. 'The schools will open on 8 November. What bliss! Another month's holiday.'

(Luciano was unable to go back to that school in Vicenza. In just a few weeks, 'peaceful' Monteviale turned into a dangerous trap for males born after 8 September and for known Jews in the area. Later, the small village of my childhood became one of the main centres of resistance in the Veneto: today its square has a plaque commemorating the residents who were shot there. The first surname in the list is Baruffato, the family who had run the town's only sizeable guesthouse since time immemorial; a squad of Fascists and Germans brandishing submachine guns burst into it one day in the winter of '44.)

For a long time we could not join our cousins in mourning their mother. There was still more than a year to go until the end of the war, and even then we had to wait before we could hug them. Switzerland, where they had meanwhile been living, did not allow them to go back to Italy at once. At first they lived there in a harrowing camp created for the waves of refugees, especially from East-Central Europe, who had managed to escape the deportations. Then they found lodgings in a small town close to Lugano – free, but they didn't have a penny to their name. There they waited day after day, until they eventually made their way back to Venice in late August 1945.

It was to Venice, the city of my fondest childhood memories, that I travelled with a heavy heart to meet them at last. In my diary entry for that day, which tells of our emotional reunion and the marks left on their faces by the terrible events, I unburden myself of a sense of guilt that our fates have been so different simply because they have a drop more Jewish blood than I. Moreover, I have been experiencing for a year the amusements of peacetime, while they have remained shut away with that pain inside and the indelible image of their mother swallowed up by the mountain.

MAY 1944: THE BRITISH ARE COMING

On 20 May, notwithstanding my contempt for the British, I start to become impatient: I want them to arrive.

But still they don't appear. I transcribe a witticism in Roman dialect that I saw on a wall in Trastevere: *Be patient, General Alexander, we'll come and liberate you in a few months.* In the three months since the Anzio landing they have advanced one kilometre.

2 JUNE 1944: THE AMERICANS

On 2 June, having previously paid them no heed, I finally write of the Americans. They are nicer than the British and I have never heard them mentioned at school. I say that their Fifth Army has broken through the Hitler Line and is marching victoriously towards the capital. The worst of all seem to me the 'Degaullists' (the name in use for the French troops): all mercenaries and, what is more, Negroes and Moroccans.

The names of previously unknown Roman streets are becoming familiar to me. The last German resistance is on Via Casilina, in Valmontone; the Allies are proceeding at a brisk pace, while German military convoys block Via Cassia in their retreat to the North. Aerial machine-gunners are firing on all the access roads to the capital, which no longer has any water, gas, electricity or things to eat. The provisions that we know to exist for a state of emergency, but which cannot be touched until then, have become precious.

Il Giornale d'Italia, I report, invokes the divinity of immortal Rome. But the cinema is still open: they are showing *Calafuria*, with Doris Duranti.

Finally, instead of troubling myself over the lost honour of the fatherland, I express some concern for those who cannot pay 2,200 lire for a bottle of oil or 22 lire for a single egg. Someone has told me that there have even been attacks on bakeries in popular districts. And the ATAC transport workers, as well as those at Romana Gas and the State Printing Works, have declared a general strike. I'm beginning to like the idea of rebellion – it's about time!

Fortunately there's the pope, I tell myself. I place great trust in the pontiff.

4 JUNE 1944

At dawn on 4 June, after a night interrupted by the rumble of artillery, Bianchina rings the doorbell and tells me with great excitement: 'They've arrived.'

We run down to Piazza Ungheria. A column of Americans in jeeps and armoured vehicles is winding its way along Viale Paroli from the Tiber. They laugh and sing, throwing cigarettes and bars of chocolate to the girls who cheer them. After a while, as if by a miracle, Italians appear on the back of lorries and wildly acclaim the Fascist defeat. There's even a red flag on one of them: the first I have seen in my life.

I don't take part in the euphoria. The spectacle is not to my liking: it seems undignified. I don't know who these anti-Fascists now coming into the open are, nor what they have been doing before.

In the next few days, the event about which I knew so little pours over me like a tidal wave. I record the sudden rush of news, without even trying to work out what it all means, until reports from the North about the last atrocities committed by the retreating Germans finally provide an international context in which I can gain some bearings. The chronicle of changes continues to be quite breathtaking: *Il Messagero* disappears and *Il Corriere della Sera* begins to come out; the Fosse Ardeatine massacres are discovered behind the catacombs of San Callisto; the newly formed coalition government under Bonomi includes some Communist ministers; people compromised by their relationship with the Fascist regime, including the parents of some of my friends, are arrested one after another.

In my Parioli neighbourhood, some are afraid of what might happen to them. These are 'the bourgeois' – a group to which I don't feel I belong, not only because my nearest and dearest are not Fascists, but also because the word has always been used at home with a turned-up nose, expressing a degree of contempt. Thousands of times I have heard Mother say that someone or other is 'so bourgeois'! She probably meant to say 'petty bourgeois', but to skip the extra adjective also indicated that the person in question was conformist, provincial and bigoted. We are not like that: our lives are more irregular and have a link to Trieste and Central Europe. Money has nothing to do with it, still less our place in society.

Only when I became a member of the PCI was it suggested to me that, as a bourgeois, I could not be a true revolutionary; the proletariat was resolute because it had nothing to lose but its chains, whereas I would never be prepared to risk everything.

I suffered a lot and felt ashamed when my joining the PCI made me bourgeois: that is, the same as the residents of Parioli. That is also why I rushed headlong into political militancy: to gain forgiveness for myself.

5 JUNE 1944: *L'ITALIA LIBERA*

The paper that Nino brings home, *L'Italia Libera*, is the organ of the Partito d'Azione. The headline on 5 June is: 'Rome returns to Italy'. In its pages I read for the first time – and then record in my diary with wonder and a little emotion – the names of the 'anti-Fascist martyrs': Leone Ginzburg and Pilo Albertelli.* The list will continue over the coming days.

Their biographies speak of prison, internal exile and then the Resistance – a world and a history that I am only now beginning to observe from the threshold.

Pilo Albertelli became the new name of the Liceo Umberto I, in the Esquilino district of Rome. Six or seven years later, a boy from the school introduced himself to me at a meeting of the first secondary school units of the Communist Youth Federation, for which I had responsibility; he wore short trousers and wanted to join the organization on an individual basis. It was Mario Tronti, who would become the main theoretician of *operaismo* and author of the well-known book *Operai e capitale* [Workers and Capital]. Because of his background at Pilo Albertelli, a kind of conditioned reflex on my part still associates him with that first issue of *L'Italia Libera*.

The same *L'Italia Libera* – whether as publicity or simply as a piece of advice – recommended buying Duplex cookers on the grounds that they could also use wood as fuel (a crucial feature at the time, given that there was no gas supply). I made a note of this, almost gleefully, because a fire burning tree branches from the garden reminded me of holidays in the mountains.

---

* The intellectuals Leone Ginzburg (1904–44) and Pilo Albertelli (1907–44), co-founders of the Partito d'Azione, were arrested by the Gestapo in February–March 1944. Ginzburg died soon afterwards in prison from the effects of torture, while Albertelli was among those murdered in the Fosse Ardeatine.

THE 'FUSIONISTS'

After some leanings towards the Partito d'Azione, and partly because they had a real Sardinian like him in their ranks, Nino decided to throw in his lot with the Socialists. But he didn't want to know about the Socialist leader Pietro Nenni, who was organizing many joint meetings with the Communists and generally seemed too close to them. Apart from the fear that both parties inspired in my relatives from Trieste, they all struck me as rather confused. In my diary I mention that Nino thinks it important to beware of the *fusionisti*: that is, of those who would like the Socialist PSI and the PCI to fuse into a single party. Although nothing would ever come of that project, Nino therefore threw in his lot with the Socialists around Giuseppe Saragat, even before the expulsion of the Left from the national unity government.

JULY 1944

Now there is a sort of government called the CLN [the National Liberation Council], formed of the Resistance parties including the Communists.

Everything is being founded anew – even the Bar Association. This morning Nino went to its first meeting in the courts and was very enthusiastic.

In the last few days a Union of Italian Students has also been founded, at the [Liceo] Visconti, but I know little about it.

9 AUGUST 1944: FIFTEEN YEARS OLD

By the time I turn fifteen, on 9 August, a lot of things have happened. University students have held many meetings, about which older friends keep me informed. I very much liked a film I saw at the reopened Bernini cinema: Charlie Chaplin's *The Gold Rush*. There's a new black market at the Campo dei Fiori.

I don't take part in much. I've only just finished the fourth year at school and wouldn't know where to go and nose around. I am still shy of politics, and self-absorbed. Before anything else, I have to prove to myself that I am afraid of nothing; that seems to me the prerequisite for facing life. So I creep out at night when everyone in the house is asleep. My room is on the ground floor, with a French window that opens into the garden, and from there it is easy to climb over into the street without risking the noisy gate. Obviously a curfew is in force, but I have a kitchen knife with me – to defend myself in all eventualities.

Each time I press on a little further – beyond Via Mangili, beyond Valle Giulia. On the third night I almost get as far as Piazza di Siena and my blood runs cold when I spot a Military Police jeep in the distance. I hide behind a bush, then return home heart in mouth.

I am so wrapped up in myself and in analysing my responses to fear that I am unaware of the risks of writing everything in my diary; I have never even bothered to shut it up in a box. The next day, therefore, I find a padlock on the window and am unable to go out. Without saying a word, my unduly curious mother has taken steps to protect me – more from rape than from a soldier's bullet.

AUGUST 1944: THE APICELLAS, FUTURE MORETTIS

I decide to profit from the war to end the boredom of secondary school. As it is not possible to go on holiday in the summer of 1944, I am able to study for the school-leaving exams in October and finally move on to the longed-for *liceo*. This will be almost like at university – a condition that will wrench me away from childhood and open up the possibility of moving in new circles. I'll be able to meet big boys and, who knows, perhaps even find love.

But I have to take private lessons, since there are subjects about which I know next to nothing.

My friend Marina, whose ultra-Fascist mother ended up in the Coltano internment camp, recommends a teacher called Apicella to me for mathematics, and her daughter Agata (a recent graduate) for Greek and Latin. In this way I can kill two birds with one stone; a single return journey across town instead of two represents a great advantage in Rome that summer, where public transport is not yet up and running again.

In fact, the long cycle ride from Parioli to Via Morgagni, where the Apicellas live, wins me much more than two birds. What I learn in their house goes well beyond mathematics and ancient languages. It is an anti-Fascist family, after all, and their anti-Fascism is much more *engagé* than in my home.

I can't help smiling when I think how chance – indeed, the suggestion of a Fascist family – has landed me there. Agata later became the mother of the filmmaker Nanni Moretti and the literary theorist Franco Moretti; and her sister Olga became the wife of Valentino Gerratana, who, together with Trombadori and Salinari, commanded the PCI's military forces in Rome during the occupation and went on to edit the works of Gramsci.

In my diary, I relate with passionate wonder how my muddled pieces of knowledge began to acquire a clearer form in the Apicella home, and how the events of the turbulent early months after the Liberation somehow took on a systematic shape. For the first time Communists, Socialists and the Partito d'Azione (which Agata's brother Vincenzo joined) appeared to me in a different light, no longer objects of diffidence or repulsion.

The new things I learn there make me think.

AUTUMN 1944: STUPIDITY

They don't make me think enough, however. When I pass the school-leaving exam and finally make it to the *liceo* (it begins in late November), I am caught up in quite different interests, emotions and experiences, and mix with quite different groups.

I have turned fifteen and my 'grown-up' life is beginning (even though my wretched breasts have still scarcely grown and the sight of my bosomy classmates will mortify me for a long time to come).

In the two politically most interesting years of the postwar period, 1945 and 1946, I exile myself in the most shameful stupidity. My diary, though begun on a wave of political emotion following the fall of Mussolini, is filled with silly trifles. While so much is happening in Italy and the world, I write only of love and its concomitants: the newly styled 'parties', of which there are at least two or three on Saturday and Sunday, and the lives and gossip of 'the group', as we call our in-crowd on Piazza Ungheria. The Church of Saint Bellarmino, which looks over the square, is the best place to meet boys without having to speak on the telephone – something which, at that age, no one dares to do unless they are 'going out' (another expression for dating that later fell into disuse). Then there are the terrace dances, where we hear the first American songs – 'Blue Moon', 'Night and Day', 'Chattanooga Choo Choo', and especially 'Cheek to Cheek' (great for getting physically close to boys, as we would never have dared to do otherwise).

After a while I switch to the group at the back of my house on Piazza don Minzoni (which has only just stopped being called Piazza dei Martiri fascisti). They even elect me Miss '103 Red', after the name of the first trolleybuses back in service – Red as distinct from the '103 Black', which runs along Viale Parioli.

From there I gravitate towards the group that hangs out near the sunny wall supporting the red-coloured Faculty of Architecture, which is in a street that will later be called Via Gramsci, no less. This represents real upward mobility for me, since the people in this group are a little more adult and their political–cultural stature is greater than on Piazza Ungheria; nearly all of them will end up in the PCI in the late Forties.

Love, to tell the truth, does not come my way. I talk and talk of it, asking myself what it is all about. But although sexual impulses come with adolescence, they find no place in my diary chronicles.

After a long time spent wishing for it, I finally 'go out' with Michele. He's studying medicine and is a very serious type. It takes months for him to notice my existence, but in the end I succeed. It doesn't last long, though, because I suddenly get worried that it'll be until death do us part. So, after I have filled page after page with 'Do I love him or don't I?', we split up. Sex: we don't even think about it. Even kissing seems a problem, and our old friend Padre Stefanu, in whom I still confide although I am not religious, makes things more complicated. 'You shouldn't kiss', he says, 'you should keep yourself for the one who will be the man of your life.'

The diary expresses my puzzlement: 'But how can I know who that will be if I have to run away from every man as soon as I've met him?'

JANUARY 1945

Some boys are leaving for the front again. This time it's the other way round: they are enlisting with the troops who are now our allies. They are mostly students, some of them from Il Tasso. But it's said that there are also workers among them.

I like that: it's a way out of passivity, even if I don't really understand where they are being posted.

A cinema club has been set up. I think it'll be screening films we couldn't see because of Fascism. I shall become a member. It reminds me of the Guf cinema in Verona, where I saw so many wonderful films.

FEBRUARY 1945: LA MARCIGLIANA

You only really notice nature when you are an adolescent. You feel the seasons on your skin; they suddenly show their first signs and divide your life up into clear chunks of time. This must have something to do with the school calendar, or perhaps it is simply due to hormonal factors. But the fact is that you are also more curious: you haven't yet given up trying to understand the universe and why we find ourselves in it. So you look more at the rest of creation, searching for a logical connection.

At the same time, your first reading of books in the Romantic tradition – which exalt nature and instinct as good and treat civilization as evil – arouse a wish to lose yourself in nature. In the diary I speak continually of nature, calling it 'she' and yearning to immerse myself in it, to abandon city and friends for a retreat in the country. In the end, I justify my persistence in the midst of people by inventing the idea that 'she' has conferred on me 'the human essence precisely so that I should live and have as many experiences as possible, since each one brings an expansion of knowledge and therefore of consciousness, and hence a way out of confusion'.

To find nature, I went as soon as I could to a property that some distant cousins had at the gates of Rome, in the Marcigliana nature reserve. My thinking was that they could take me back in their van when they brought some eggs and butter (for us too) that were unobtainable in the city. What have since developed as suburban areas were then given over to horses and fields, visited only now and then by herds of cattle and flocks of sheep.

I rode off alone on horseback for hours at a time, down to the banks of the Tiber or towards the hills, crossing the ancient Via Salaria down which no one had travelled for so long. I fell off frequently, because the horses had only crupperless Maremma saddles and I was used to English ones. But it was really magnificent.

11 FEBRUARY 1945: AN IMPORTANT LOVE

My second love, an architecture student, involved more of a commitment. I got to know him in circumstances which – on re-reading the account in my diary – leave me dumbfounded. It was at a Carnival party, in Gulienetti's house on Via dei Legionari (another Fascist street name, which they had not got round to changing); the date was 11 February 1945, when the war was still raging on every front and partisans were being slaughtered a few hundred kilometres away, on the Gothic Line. And we were in Parioli celebrating the Roman Carnival – in fancy dress, to boot.

I fell madly in love with Carlo Aymonino precisely because he looked fantastic disguised as an officer in the Royal Guard. I, on the other hand, was feeling downhearted because, while my girlfriends were dressed as little princesses, I wore a Finnish costume from the collection of traditional clothes that my aunts from Trieste had brought for me over the years from their exotic trips abroad.

I looked like a sack, but the royal officer generously 'bought' me during a mindless auction game. It left me feeling quite shaken.

It still took nearly a year before we got together, despite the fact that during the New Year holiday of 1945–46 – the first great postwar skiing trip – a dozen of us, if not more, slept in one room in a freezing mountain shelter at Campocatino, southeast of Rome.

We made up our minds only when his father's sudden death in January 1946 loosened our inhibitions, owing both to his need for comfort and to my wish to provide it. He wanted to be a painter, as I did too, and that was a major factor holding our relationship together.

Nevertheless, that story too was soon over, although it picked up several times over the next few years. Again the main reason for the break was my terror that we would be grandparents together – and besides, in 1947 other interests were beginning to attract me. But our friendship always endured, so much so that, on the fifth anniversary of that shameful Maundy Thursday in 1945 when we first met at Via dei Legionari, Carlo sent me a letter announcing that he had overcome his final hesitations and decided to join the PCI (almost three years after me). It was a beautiful and important letter, which I still have in my possession. For it testifies not only to a personal bond but also to the huge significance that the decision to become Communists had for us.

'I wanted to give you a present on this anniversary', he writes, 'but then I thought that the finest and certainly the most substantive present would be to inform you of my decision to join the Party. A present, a debt to you – but above all to myself. Perhaps it will seem a little "Mexican" to combine in a single date two such important but also such different events. But it has served me as a fixed reference point, because only in this way could I overcome the absurd, illogical and therefore immoral situation in which I found myself, and which meant that there was no longer any real reason for me not to join the Party. At this moment I am immensely happy. I know – and I will realize more and more in the future – that it is the most important date in my life, and I am happy that it is joined to the date on which we first met. In essence, there's something of a cause-and-effect process! Whatever may be the future relations between us, the positive and negative moments, I shall always be grateful for what you have done to gradually clarify my "human condition", to push it to develop in a logical and coherent direction. I hope you may one day say as much of me.'

PAINTING

During that period, which in retrospect I might define as 'transitional', little reading but many pictures featured in my diary. The only cultural interest left to me was painting – not so much an interest, more an obsession. This was fuelled by the company of architecture students, beginning with Carlo, quite a few of whom had a smouldering ambition to become an artist. I too had always wanted to paint, and I drew whenever I could. Indeed, I couldn't say whether I sought out painters because I wanted to become one too, or whether I thought that was what I did in life because I spent all my time chatting with them on the wall beneath the Faculty of Architecture, just a stone's throw from the Gallery of Modern Art that had opened its doors again in the autumn of '45.

When I think about it today, it seems amazing that painting played a unique, unprecedented role in those early post-Fascist years. The fact is that Fascism and provincialism had denied us knowledge of modern painting even more than of literature (a few works such as Vittorini's *Americana* collection had got through to us). And it became a symbol of liberation, because in those years it was closely bound up with politics.

I would even say that I came to politics through exhibitions of new artists, both foreign and Italian.

I discovered the first 'revolutionary' shows in Autumn '44; they were actually organized by political parties! In September 'Art against Barbarism' opened at the Galleria di Roma (previously under a cloud after it exhibited a canvas by Renato Guttuso, *Shooting in the Countryside*, said to represent the killing of the anti-Franco poet Garcia Lorca, whose work I immediately tried to track down). Sponsored by *L'Unità* on behalf of the Communist Party, it featured works by Mafai, Guttuso, Mirko and Leoncillo. Another exhibition, organized there by *L'Italia Libera* on behalf of the Rome Committee of the Youth Federation of the Partito d'Azione, was limited to artists under thirty-five. The programme notes (which I faithfully copied into my diary because a couple of architecture students, including the one who 'bought' me at the Carnival party, were among the participants) explain that the age barrier is designed 'among other things, to test the damage caused by twenty years of restricted artistic knowledge and forced isolation from what is alive in global artistic trends. In a period that should see a revival of the Italian spirit, the sponsors thought it fitting to focus attention on one of its most characteristic aspects: Italy's instinct and talent for art.'

Many of the hopefuls for this revival of the Italian spirit were very young: Aymonino, Busiri, Maselli, Vespigniani, 'not yet twenty years old'.

In November it was the turn of Christian Democracy to hold its exhibition of paintings.

At the Galleria di Valle Giulia, the little neoclassical palace built for the World Fair of 1911 (Grandfather printed the catalogue on his press), there was an enterprising and critical young woman who later became its director: Palma Bucarelli. In a striking *coup de main*, she displayed her personal selection from the works 'evacuated' to Caprarola in the Cimini Hills: an exquisitely chosen sample of the period straddling Fascism and post-Fascism. This opened up a generation from the 'difficult years' – painters like Carrà, Campigli, Morandi and Rosai, who came out of Margherita Sarfatti's salon* but often ended up well beyond it. I hadn't had a chance to discover them before, so for us everything was now appearing all at once.

Some of the painters presented by Bucarelli had learned from Impressionism, while a number of younger ones had heard in the Thirties how much was ripening across the frontier, in the 'adult world' that for us was unquestionably France. (We hadn't yet discovered America.) I had also seen some of these at the Galleria di Roma. Although they were anti-Fascist artists, their works were less explicitly denunciatory since they dated from before the war and had been acquired in the Thirties: Casorati, Morlotti, above all the Roman school of Scipione and Mafai. I hadn't known they existed, but now they suddenly became my heroes; I seemed to find in their paintings what I took to be modernism.

---

* Margherita Sarfatti (1880–1961): literary figure and art critic, one-time mistress of Mussolini, who organized a number of exhibitions of contemporary Italian painting. She fell into disgrace in 1934.

15 MARCH 1945

Roosevelt is dead. They stopped our classes this morning to tell us the news. No school tomorrow. But was this Roosevelt really so important for a national day of mourning to be declared? I know little about him, but it irritates me that homage must be paid to someone who isn't Italian: or rather, that there seems to be no Italian to whom homage can be paid.

20 APRIL 1945

I am horrified, I can't believe it. The cover of a new weekly crime magazine, Crimen, documentario settimanale di criminologia, *shows a German soldier surrendering, while inside there are mug shots of major criminals. A few pages, headed 'Criminal Museum', contain photos with explanations: Vidkun Abraham Lauritz Quisling, Norwegian, hangman of his country; Marcel [sic] Doriot, Communist renegade, founder of French Fascism; Degrelle, leader of the Belgian Fascists; Giuseppe Pizzirani, head of the Fascist movement during the occupation of Rome; Gino Bardi, who ran the prison at Palazzo Braschi; and now the horrifying one: Elda Norchi née Simeoni, pharmacist, leader of the Roman Republican Fascists, arrested by the Allied police. The mother of my friend Marina.*

26 APRIL 1945

The German occupation is over. The partisans rose up and meanwhile the British and Americans arrived. This time the war should be finished once and for all.

War

29 APRIL 1945

I went to Piazza Santi Apostoli to see the celebrations organized by the CLN. There were lots of people and all the new parties gave speeches. There was special applause for Nenni, who announced a Republic and a Constitution.

Nothing was said about Trieste, although all the papers continue to speak of its fate.

30 APRIL 1945

An extraordinary film, an American animated cartoon: Snow White and the Seven Dwarfs.

1 MAY 1945

Yesterday, Yugoslav troops under Marshal Tito entered Trieste, the only remaining city under German occupation. Great joy at home and also great fear: the Titoists will be looking for revenge.

There was a demonstration with huge numbers of people at Piazza del Popolo, for what is called 'Labour Day'. One of those who spoke was a friend of Nino's: the lawyer Berlinguer, also from Sassari.

2 MAY 1945

It seems that New Zealand troops have crossed the Piave and the Isonzo and are marching towards Istria, having liberated Monfalcone. Twenty kilometres from Trieste they apparently encountered Tito's troops, who are supposed to have said that Trieste must remain Yugoslav and that they have a right to it in the name of democracy. My aunts are trembling.

It is being said that Hitler shot himself at No. 77 Wilhelmstrasse, in Berlin.

4 MAY 1945

Today was an earthshaking day; I'm totally confused at the end of it.

But let's take things in order. For a couple of days, the pupils at the liceo *had been organizing a march to protest against the Communists and Socialists, who allegedly want to abandon Trieste to the Yugoslavs. I went to listen, thinking that Grandfather would turn in his grave if he knew that, having taken the city from the Austrians, we were now going to hand it over to Tito. They decided on the 4th, and on the chosen morning (that is, today) virtually no one showed up in class. The teachers and headmaster stood at the main door on Via Sicilia, but fortunately they said nothing and even seemed to be in agreement with us. There were so many of us when we formed up in columns. I placed myself in the front row: it seemed to be my duty, again on account of Grandfather.*

When we were about to reach the place of the rally, I saw that Piazza Esedra was already chock-a-block. Marches from other schools were pouring into it and we expressed our satisfaction that things were turning out so well. But as we moved forward, we noticed that those already in the square were not actually students: they were workers, and pretty muscular ones at that. They had no intention of welcoming us there. In fact, they were constructing a barrier; scuffles broke out, people got knocked around, I was hit on the back by a flagpole – sadly it bore the royal emblem, brought by someone or other, certainly not by us from Il Tasso – and the pain forced me to sit on the steps of the colonnade.

The clashes dragged on: some of us ran away, some went down Via Nazionale towards the Altar of the Fatherland, where the demonstration was supposed to reach its climax. At some point shooting could be heard and we were all afraid. Just as I too was on the point of leaving, a small group appeared and put together a kind of meeting; the speakers stood at the top of the right side of the flight of steps. They were Communists and Socialists: the best informed, people whispered to me. They had come straight from the nearby PCI headquarters, which had apparently been attacked by an armed gang under a certain Captain Penna Nera; I knew nothing about him, but it seems he had been at the head of our demonstration. I stopped to listen, a good distance away. I confess that, as they spoke, I was gradually becoming convinced that what they said made sense. They referred to the atrocities – I had never heard of them – which the Fascists committed against the Slovenes way back in the Twenties, chasing them from their land and forcing them to take refuge in Slovenia. And to the massacres during the occupation of Yugoslavia – another unknown chapter. Then a man from Trieste by the name of Jacchía also gave a speech, saying that the only way to redeem the Italians was to do as his mother did when she fought for two years alongside the Yugoslav partisans against the Fascists and Nazis. Other speakers said they didn't want Trieste to stop being Italian, but that the Yugoslavs too had their rights, after everything the Italian Fascists (that is, the Italians) did. The problem could be solved only by the free peoples of the two countries, and meanwhile they saluted the partisans, both Italian and Yugoslav, who had liberated Trieste.*

At the end I too went towards Piazza Venezia. There the students from the Cavour liceo, who are said to be left-wing, joined the by now highly confused marches. Scuffles continued at the Altar of the Fatherland, but it

---

* That is: Captain Black Feather.

was not clear who was fighting whom. Someone shouted that the Unknown Soldier was a son of the people. I think he meant that he was on the Left. And the ones who were doing the shouting also beat up some Fascists, ex-repubblichini, who for their part tried as hard as they could to scream against those who were 'selling the fatherland'. An announcement kept being repeated amid the hubbub. 'Comrade Remo Cantoni, a worker at Manzolini, has had a wrist broken by the Blackshirts, and in the commotion he has also lost his bicycle. Please help him find it.'*

I bumped into my friend Claudia in the crowd and we went together down Via del Corso, because it was said that Italian troops were due to march past (on whose side?). But hours passed and there was no sign of them.

I returned home exhausted. And very puzzled. I remembered that at home Slovenes were called schavi *[Slavonians]: that is,* schiavi *[slaves]. And that, more or less, is how they were treated – with contempt.*

These are things I have never thought about. I should go and see those Communists at Il Tasso to understand things better.

5 MAY 1945

I read the papers avidly today. I even looked at L'Unità *and* Avanti, *to find out what they were saying about our demonstration. They tell a story that is completely new to me. Apparently there were some disguised Fascists in our ranks – even a parachutist, Lieutenant Spinello, who shot and wounded the worker Cantoni in the incident that triggered the clashes. They also blame the headmasters, including at Il Tasso, for behaving in an educationally unsound manner, in effect encouraging students to stay away from school and join the demonstration. But then*

---

* Former fighters of the Repubblica di Salò.

they say that the organizers included a 'Fronte Giuliano per l'integrità dell'Italia', a body which, though wishing Trieste to be Italian, does not follow the nationalists in trying only to sabotage the peace. So, they weren't just Fascists on our side? We weren't completely wrong to take part? In any case, left-wing students also played a role.

To be on the safe side, L'Unità headlines 'Students and workers fraternize at the Altar of the Fatherland in a great patriotic demonstration. From Esedra to Vittoriano the provocateurs remained isolated.' They might have fraternized with the ones from Cavour, but truly all we got from them were beatings.

But apart from these incongruities, I also read some things that are correct: for example, that we ought to put right an injustice, that what is needed is a solution which satisfies everyone and will not compromise future relations of fraternity between the Italian and Yugoslav peoples. For this reason, one should not get mixed up with people who use Trieste for a nationalistic, semi-Fascist campaign reminiscent of D'Annunzio. Who knows what Grandfather would have said of it all?

The fact is that the situation in Trieste is more than confused. Italy has now been liberated, but that city has not yet been completely. It seems that there are still bands of Germans. The manoeuvres are unclear, but it is evident that attempts are being made to prevent the Yugoslavs from taking full possession of the city before the British and Americans arrive.

2. PEACE

Today the war officially ended. The British radio seems to have said that King George himself announced it at 14:09. I don't feel any great emotion, because for me the war ended a year ago and I haven't really suffered personally during these last terrible months.

Meeting at the University (I played truant and went there). At least five thousand students. Attempt to leave and go back to the Altar of the Fatherland, although I'm no longer quite sure why. We didn't go there, however, because the police blocked the gates. There were also some city policemen on horseback.

Meanwhile the government, including Minister Togliatti, received the Julian Liberation Committee, which told them not to be insensitive to its cry of pain. Bonomi spoke of his happiness after the First World War, when the tricolour was raised on the Torre di San Giusto in Trieste. He recognized that the Fascists committed grave deeds, but said that their guilt is not ours. However, the Yugoslavs do not seem to be of the same opinion.

12 MAY 1945

Trieste has been liberated at last and an agreement has been signed between General Alexander and Marshal Tito: the Allies will be in charge of the port, the Titoists of the city areas. But here – to the dread of our Triestine relatives, for whom they were friends – it seems that two ship-owners have been arrested: Baron Economo Tripcovich and Cosulich.

14 MAY 1945

Archbishop Damaskinos has gone to Rhodes to celebrate the island's return to the Greek motherland. The French have occupied the Western valleys of Piedmont. The war is scarcely over and everyone is already arguing over borders.

15 MAY 1945

The first Congress of Students has been held at the University, but we liceo *students were excluded. Apparently they want a reform of the educational system. Why not us?*

Concetto Marchesi from Padua – a professor with a masculinized female first name, who is said to be very well known and to have been a partisan – suggested that the Congress should organize university camps in barracks for ex-servicemen and evacuees, as well as colleges where young workers can take crash courses to catch up on their education. I think that's a good idea: but if everyone studies, who will work? Actually, though, why should I study instead of going to work?

I'm beginning to have doubts about my privileges, which until now I've taken for granted as if they were a fact of nature. Of course I've used the word equality thousands of times, but I've never drawn inspiration from it for ideas of any consequence, never applied it to myself.

17 MAY 1945

Nino brought home a copy of La Settimana, *a paper that has only recently appeared. It also has a drawing by the famous Guttuso. It has made a big impression on me, because this issue is entirely devoted to the Resistance (about which I know nothing). It bears the title: 'Italy Has Woken!' Is that 'Scipio's helmet' now upon the head of the 'bandits'?*[*]

A man with a curious name, Felice Platone, relates 'our war', and says that it began well before 1940. In the end it's a convincing story, because he speaks of the imprisoned, murdered and exiled: Gramsci, Rosselli,[†] *Matteotti,*[‡] *Don Minzoni.*[§] *There is also a photographic chronicle starting on 26 July 1943, the very day on which I began this diary in Riccione. There are the displays of joy for the downfall of Mussolini, like the one*

---

[*] 'Il Canto degli Italiani', the Italian national anthem, contains the lines: 'Brothers of Italy, / Italy has woken, / Bound Scipio's helmet / Upon her head.' The reference to Scipio evokes his role in defeating the forces of Hannibal, the Carthaginian invader of Roman Italy. 'Bandits' was, of course, the Fascist and Nazi term for Italian partisans.

[†] Nello Rosselli, historian and artist, was visiting his brother Carlo on the French Riviera in June 1937 (where he was recovering from wounds incurred in the Spanish Civil War), when both were assassinated by French Fascists at the behest of Mussolini.

[‡] Giacomo Matteotti: Socialist political leader who was kidnapped and murdered by Fascists in June 1924, shortly after he spoke in the Italian parliament denouncing their use of violence and electoral fraud.

[§] Giovanni Minzoni: anti-Fascist priest murdered by Fascist *squadristi* in August 1923.

I witnessed. In another you can see a banner: 'He wanted to be Caesar, he ended up Vespasian.' Then come the photos of patriots who fell in Naples during the Four Days at the end of September, on the eve of the Allies' entry into the city. It runs through all eighteen months of the Resistance, and by the end I also know what happened when Milaide became involved, at Via Tasso.

So, there were people who held in their hands the threads of the period before Fascism and the period before the war, and who tried to connect them up with what came afterwards, or rather with what had to be done to make it happen – a tissue with a certain logic. They were not like the people I have met until now, beginning with the adults closest to me, for whom events seem to have no causes or effects and therefore always remain implausible, unexpected, no more than a rolling forward without any meaning.

Also in La Settimana there are pictures of a Communist, Sereni, a Christian Democrat, Marazza, a Socialist, Morandi, a Partito d'Azione leader, Valiani, and a Liberal, Arpesani. They make up the CLN delegation from North Italy, which came to Rome to meet the people from Central Italy with a view to forming a government. Also many photos of hanged partisans, many girls with long, copious hair and always, for some reason, a raincoat, who are embracing their rifle. (In that case, could I too have been a partisan, even though I'm a woman?)

---

* *Vespasiano*: a public urinal – an allusion to the fate of Mussolini's corpse when it was displayed in public following his execution on 28 April 1945.

Peace

20 MAY 1945

As a filler for Seven Sweethearts, *which was on at the Cinema Moderno, they showed a documentary on the concentration camps in Germany. Could all that have possibly happened?*

9 AUGUST 1945

I'm turning sixteen and a bomb has just been exploded that could apparently destroy the whole world: two thousand times bigger than the British 'Grand Slam', which already seemed enormous. The Americans dropped it on a Japanese city, Hiroshima, where everyone seems to be dead – hundreds of thousands.

It's hot: 42 degrees. Must be because of the bomb.

SUMMER 1945: RETURN TO VENICE

My silly little world went sky high at Ferragosto.* Only now am I discovering a side of life that I only used to suspect but never really took into consideration.

I discovered it in its ugliest version, for which I was completely unprepared – and I did so not through direct experience but only as a spectator. I'm not sure whether that is for better or worse.

It happened when the old chauffeur Oscar arrived in Rome from Trieste to take back my aunts. (Though still in bad shape, the Italian roads could be driven on.) The very day after the Liberation, my refugee relatives managed to get in touch with the people looking after the hillside villa by the sea and, to their amazement, discovered not only that nothing had been destroyed, but that the

---

* The mid-August public holiday, on 15 August.

Germans – whose headquarters were located there – had made some improvements: a swimming pool dug out next to the tennis court. (In my diary I make a wry face: such good fortune, amid so many tragedies, seems to me an injustice.)

Preceded northward by Aunt Anna and Uncle Vico (the 'young ones'), the octogenarians also long to return home. They suggest that I go with them: they'll drop me off in Venice, where Silvia (Aunt Ester's granddaughter) spent the last two years of the war. Likeable enough, though a spoilt and whimsical heiress, Silvia is married to a pretty fascistic Aryan, who bestowed his pure name to protect the businesses of the Liebman-Modiano family and to keep his young wife safe from racial persecution.

Naturally I was happy with the proposal: my Ascoli cousins were due to arrive any day from Switzerland, so I could meet them even earlier if I got to Venice before them. And meanwhile I'd be able to see my childhood friends, my beloved city, the Lido beach.

After an emotional journey through the Furlo Pass, the bombed villages of the Marches and Romagna and a hold-up for hours at Alfonsine (where not all those killed in the last tremendous battle to cross the Po had yet been buried), I realized on my first evening in Venice that I had landed in a different world. Silvia's home attracted a motley crowd of ex-Fascists in hiding, collaborators with the new authorities, officers linked to the Allied General Staff, adventurers, and ladies looking for a job, however temporary. Wars produce such human dust behind the lines, and before disappearing in peacetime conditions it remains hovering for a while, unsure which road to take. The large house behind Piazza San Marco, where I found myself thinking it was still like the houses I knew, served as their life raft (along with the just reopened Grand Hotel) during those weeks. For me it was like going to see a film for adults only.

They got me drunk on the second day, so much that I slept for the next twenty-four hours. Or perhaps (in my ignorance, I didn't even suspect it at the time) they added a few drops of something else: not to abuse me – no, they would never have done that – but to remove a possible witness to their little night-time orgies and the desperate games of poker played out in their gambling den.

I understood, yet everything was somehow blurred. I felt frightened but also a little curious, and above all proud to be experiencing something new (as at the time of my mother's marriage annulment), to be acquiring a greater knowledge of the world than that of girls of the same age as myself.

Rather than rush back to Rome, I decided to stay a while in the house and ignore the life there – without mentioning anything to my parents or aunts, in case they made me leave. I went out early in the morning to go to the Lido, came back very late, and sneaked into my room without passing through the lounge. All this was possible because, instead of my old childhood friends with their rigid family timetable, I stumbled across a species of boys and girls previously unknown to me: the Milanesi.

Super-rich Milanese, as free as little birds, who ate out and went clubbing until late in a few places that had reopened. They wore the most expensive gear – who knows how they managed to get their hands on it.

There were also a lot of parties in that late summer of '45 in Venice – all very exotic, of course; my Venetians would never have shown their faces there. At one of them I met the crown prince of Afghanistan (so I was told, but God knows if it was true), who, having danced with me all evening, sent two of his officials to tell me: 'His Highness would like to invite you onto his yacht to take a little trip on the lagoon.' My curiosity aroused, I immediately accepted the offer; perhaps my life would then have been spent in a harem, instead of in Communist branch organizations, if a young liaison officer I had met in the previous days had not intervened to take me by the arm and haul me away from the party. 'Go straight home', he said to me, with an authority I hadn't expected of him, but to which I bowed without batting an eyelid. 'In the morning, I'll pick you up and take you to where you come from.'

So, the next day my fine Venetian life was rudely interrupted, and a military vehicle astonished my Ascoli cousins in Monteviale by depositing me at their doorstep. Paoletta and Luciano had already been there for several days, having returned from Switzerland via Venice. They hadn't wanted to stop at all in the city, where there was no longer anything they could call theirs, but had hurried on to find the memory of their mother in the large country house near Vicenza from which they had fled during the war.

I remained there quite a long time, since that year no one knew for sure when the schools would reopen. Weeks of dreams and absurd projects: but I'd have done anything not to return to the second year of *liceo* in my little old world. In my diary, I write of stowing away in the hold of a ship bound for distant shores – I had heard people in Venice speak of such places. Everything seemed possible: you just had to want it.

Obviously I didn't want it enough, because late October saw me back in Rome, really and truly caught up in the round of parties that raged through the winter of '45–'46.

30 SEPTEMBER 1945

At the Quirino, where the first postwar cinema festival is taking place, there's a wonderful film called Les Enfants du Paradis. *An Italian one, by a young director, also had a big impact on me because it tells an (apparently true) story that happened in Rome in '44 – the city where I too lived that year – but which I would never have imagined was possible:* Rome, Open City.

They have named the mayor of Rome: a prince, no less, Doria Pamphili. But they say he's an anti-Fascist prince.

10 NOVEMBER 1945: SECOND YEAR OF *LICEO*

The schools are reopening. I'm in the second year of liceo.

All the painters and writers [I note with some amazement] are joining the PCI: even Vittorini, who edited the Americana *collection, the book I liked the most. Also Quasimodo: the one who translated the Greek poems we studied at school.*

THE HINNA WORKSHOP

I'll be a painter, I'm sure of it. That's what Grandfather wanted to be, but he never succeeded. So in the afternoon I go with my friend Giacinta to the Villa Strohl-Fern, beyond the steps of Valle Giulia, where old Professor Hinna has his workshop. He doesn't teach us anything interesting; in fact, I who already know about Picasso, and certainly about the Impressionists, find it pretty dull. But there are nude models, and the painters there work in peace, concentrating hard. I'm good at drawing and everyone pays me compliments, but I realize that I don't have a feel for colour. (Afterwards I'll give the whole thing up.) Meanwhile I go to all the exhibitions: there are beginning to be quite a lot of them and they open up a new world. I'm hungry for suggestions and tricks of the trade. I wonder how they get people who don't paint interested in their paintings.

18 NOVEMBER 1945

Yesterday was International Students' Day, in memory of a massacre committed by the Germans at Prague University in 1939.

The most interesting thing I've seen up to now: the Liberation exhibition, at Palazzo Venezia. There are loads of photos, documents and paintings that illustrate what happened in '44 and '45. In Val d'Ossola a republic was even proclaimed in the liberated zone: some of its stamps were on display! There were many letters written by partisans condemned to death.

4 JANUARY 1946

'The fusion between the PCI and PSI really seems to be on. Nenni said as much when he greeted the Communist Congress being held in Rome, at the University. He said that burying unity between the two parties is like burying the working class.'

Politics – to judge by my diary for these months – seems to have been arousing great curiosity on my part, but I can't get my bearings among the different parties; I have only second-hand information about them from older schoolmates. I see that I need to understand more, but I remain stuck halfway, curious about my new friends and what is happening, but still not used to reading the papers regularly. The call of the milieu in which I grew up is still strong, and the people in it do not seem to notice what is staring them in the face.

'At school', I write, 'someone speaks of Togliatti, who is the leader of the Communists and says that the fall of Fascism has left a still unfilled void in young people who haven't yet understood that "our same ideal" animates them. He sounds like someone who understands. But this "same" is a little indecipherable: What do we have in common when thinking of a new fatherland?

'We all speak of the vote for women. It seems to me impossible that they haven't had it up to now. And yet, when I speak with friends, I discover that nearly all the male ones think women lose their femininity if they do the same things as men. They criticize me for this, saying that I'm too keen on not being a woman. In fact, they call me sarcastically "our friend [*amico*] Lucianina" – someone with whom they don't go out but debate. And they add – much to my annoyance – that I "know nothing about the animal *masculus vulgaris*". Perhaps I'll never find a husband. Patience.'

14 FEBRUARY 1946: A TALK ON CUBISM

'A big test; I'm still worked up.'

Perhaps the Communists decided they could take another little step in the operation of recruiting me. Anyway, having seen me show up quite regularly for talks in the circle they ran at school, and knowing that my ambition was to be painter, they asked me to give a lecture on Cubism right there. Picasso had recently joined the French Communist Party, so it was a natural request.

To tell the truth, none of us had yet seen his paintings. But Venturi had the splendid idea of making contemporary French art better known by means of an exhibition of colour prints (still hard to find in Italy) at the Galleria di Valle Giulia. He also organized an illuminating course of lectures there.

I had read about Cubism, and I had been struck (so much that I quoted it in my talk) by a remark of Gino Severini's, the only Italian painter who had lived in Paris. 'Cubism and Impressionism alike', he said, 'are turning-points of history; they have inescapable consequences that become clearer with the passing of time.'

With this scant knowledge I turned to the first assignment ever given me by the PCI: to give a talk on Cubism. I felt terrified, being all too aware of my ignorance and in awe of the elite culture flaunted by my Communist schoolmates. The diary reports days of painful preparation. And then disappointment: most of the students who attended my talk knew nothing about Cubism and openly sniggered at the contorted pictures by my idols that I showed them from the first books that had arrived from France. I hit back by quoting a sentence of Picasso's that I had come across shortly before: 'It is not the job of painting to decorate apartments. It is an instrument of offensive and defensive warfare against the enemy.'

I think that this affirmation was my first political gesture.

'There's a lot of discussion about Abstract Art,' I recorded in my diary, 'and also about Cubism and Realism. The Communists are divided: Guttuso, now a PCI member, is neorealist; Fougeron, a former Renault worker and a member of the PCF, is a non-figurative artist. I don't know what the non-Communists are, because I don't think there are any non-Communist painters.'

As for the Communists, I finally got to know one at the house of my friend Franchino De Gregorio. His mother was friendly with the artist's lover, Mimíse. 'Guttuso doesn't have the face of either a painter or a Communist. But he's simpatico', I conceded.

I understood more about the burden of Italian provincialism from an issue of the journal *Il Mercurio*, edited by Alba de Céspedes, which must have been the first political–cultural publication I acquired in my life, second-hand and late. (It was there that I came across Severini's remark, the lynchpin of my public debut.)

That issue of December 1944, which I still keep at home, has my name proudly written on the first page as a mark of ownership (not the 'Ex Libris' with a picture of a cat that adorned all of Nino's books). 'We are the only country,' I noted indignantly, having

With Anna Maria Mussolini at Lante della Rovere Elementary School, Rome, 1937–38. Luciana Castellina on extreme left of second row. The girl sitting center-right in the first row of desks is Anna Maria Mussolini.

In *marinaretta tamburina* uniform, Rome, 1936.

With her cousin, Luciano Ascoli, at Monteviale, 1937.

With her mother at Venice Lido, circa 1939.

In Zenica, Yugoslavia, during construction of the Youth Railway, 1947.

1 May 1947, Rome.

At Rome University, 1947.

Luciana Castellina in the crowd during protest demonstration after the attempt on Togliatti's life, Rome, 14 July 1948.

Arrest after Togliatti protest demonstrations, Rome, 15 July 1948.

In the Chamber of Deputies, 1977–78.

Quotidiano ecologista

Terra

Anno 80° - domenica 9 agosto 2009 - € 1.000.000   www.terranews.it

left
AVVENIMENTI

Ottanta anni di scavi
non sono bastati.
Continua a scavare
vecchia talpa...
Per il comunismo,
non per meno

TANTI AUGURI

Photomontage, 9 August 2009. Eightieth birthday present from friends.

learned it from *Il Mercurio*, 'which, along with Spain, has no gallery of contemporary art. In contrast to the volcano that is Paris!'

Il Mercurio – which I do not mention more often because it soon ceased publication – played a crucial role for me. In its now forgotten pages I was faced with questions that no one had ever posed to me before – and, most particularly, with Toti Scialoja's wicked reviews, which I have now re-read and think should be republished! On Mafai, for example, he writes with iconoclastic admiration that his 'jerky figures toss around like groups of skinned frogs scientifically leaping on the point of his brush'.[*]

I understood that there was history in the pages of *Il Mercurio* – as well as the artists' desire to find a relationship with history which, perhaps in order to escape its rigours, they had previously tried to erase. I noted down a quotation from E. T. A. Hoffmann, which Scialoja had used in presenting the *Unità* exhibition on 'Art against Barbarism', or 'Roman Artists against Nazi-Fascist Oppression': 'What artist has ever troubled himself with the political events of the day anyway? He lived only for his art, and advanced through life serving it alone. But a dark and unhappy age has seized men with its iron fist, and the pain squeezes from them sounds that were formerly alien to them.'[†] For painters, and not only for them, the turning-point was a painting that remained the symbol of its time: Picasso's *Guernica* – another canvas that we long knew only from reproductions.

Hoffmann's image is truly decisive for an understanding of those years and of us who lived through them. We were all 'seized' by

---

[*] Toti Scialoja (1914–98): a poet and painter associated with abstract art and the Roman School.

[†] David Charlton, ed., *E. T. A. Hoffmann's Musical Writings* (Cambridge: Cambridge University Press, 1989), p. 111.

history, by the reality surrounding us – even if the road ahead was slower and more tortuous for those, like myself, who had not been old enough to experience the Resistance or to be really aware of the anti-Fascist movement. (Some years later, Italo Calvino wrote that ours was not a generation of iconoclasts, of 'angry young people', because it had a keener sense than others of participating in history: 'A commitment with no let-up, lived joyfully and freely more than self-assertively.')

This new collective dimension helped me to find a way out from the circle of self-reference and even to rediscover the meaning of *patria* [fatherland] – a word I had once spelled with a capital 'P', before obliterating it as illusory rhetoric. The love I began to feel for neighbours quite remote from my social ghetto, for underprivileged people, refugees, the unemployed, ex-servicemen and martyrs, gave me back a sense of solidarity. If not *patria*, it was something resembling it. And gradually it awakened my interest in politics, which, in fact, is the opposite of navel-gazing.

20 FEBRUARY 1946

Carlo Aymonino, together with Dorazio, Perilli and Busiri, found the nerve to go to Guttuso's studio on Via Margutta. They told me they knocked for a long time but no one answered – although they were sure he was there. Then finally his angry voice. He calmed down a little when they said they were painters, and told them to come back in half an hour. They sat on a wall opposite until they saw the Countess, the famous Mimíse – his semi-secret lover I knew from Franchino – make her way*

---

* Piero Dorazio, Achille Perilli and Carlo Busiri Vici were all artists belonging to the post-war generation of painters.

*out. When they tried again, he greeted them with a smile, obviously
relying on their complicity.*

*Dorazio had brought his draft manifesto on 'Social Art' to show
him, describing it as both 'social' and 'Marxist'. Carlo didn't like it, but
apparently Guttuso discussed it for a long time. On the walls – they told
me – were three portraits he had painted: one of Stalin, one of Lenin and
one of Picasso, plus a reproduction of Cézanne's* Boy in the Red Vest.

*Guttuso readily agreed to present their exhibition, and said
that Cubism has not become known in Italy: that it will need to
pass through that experience. In Milan, he informed them, there
is already a group of young Cubists around Cassinari.* Rome –
*Guttuso said – is more dead. Carlo was very happy with the meeting,
partly because Guttuso told him that he'd seen one of his landscapes at
the young artists' exhibition sponsored by the Partito d'Azione and had
wanted to give it a prize (although the others had opposed this on the
grounds that he was too young). Then he showed them some early works,
a series on beggars. According to Carlo, he is influenced by Cubism in
many ways but is not a Cubist. And critics say of him, sarcastically, that
he's a 'Cubist in Sicilian sauce': or rather, a Sicilian 'Picassata'.*

I feel very envious that they had this meeting.

6 MARCH 1946

*At last the exhibition is happening. At the Via Margutta Artistic Circle:
Aymonino, Busiri, Dorazio, Perilli, Vespignani and a few others. I went
with them for the opening, which is called a 'vernissage', and felt very
proud to be meeting painters on display. The whole group defines itself*

---

* Bruno Cassinari: painter and sculptor active in several artistic movements of the postwar period.

in terms of 'Social Art', and there is a lot of argument about this term. Art either is art or it isn't: 'social' doesn't come into it, my Professor Hinna says. My friends reply that it is art only if it is also social; anything else is idealism. The same goes for the revolutionary intelligentsia, someone says: either it is revolutionary or it is not an intelligentsia.

Carlo got me to read the review of the exhibition in L'Unità. It contains words of praise, saying that the young artists on display seem to have understood the need to avoid moralist or didactic aesthetics and that what they must aim at is not sociality in a narrow sectarian sense but purely and simply art; if it is that, then it will also be social. It says of Carlo in particular that his paintings are excessively Guttusian.

Carlo has also exhibited at the Circle of the Socialist Youth Federation, in Via Molise, just behind Il Tasso, with more or less the same painters from the 'Social Art' group. The father of Citto Maselli (a Communist from Il Tasso) wrote the review, and everyone is very satisfied with what he wrote because he seems to be a well-known critic. In essence, he praised it as a good first sign that they distrust the beautiful and pursue the 'painful calvary of the ugly'.

8 MARCH 1946: THE FESTIVAL OF WOMEN

Sibilla Aleramo, the friend of my grandparents who used to frequent the Flaminio printing shop and went to spread literacy among the peasantry of the Pontine Fields, has been celebrating the 8th of March, which is International Women's Day. She seems to be a Communist too. I said this to Grandmother, but she wouldn't believe it. I would like to meet her.

Peace

'Hinna has died suddenly. It upsets me that his workshop may close and I will no longer have a place where I can paint in peace with live models.

'I have discovered poetry. I'm deep into Rilke. His pantheism doesn't convince me, though, because it gives a soul to everything – hence a personality that dissolves into a higher being than me. I cannot accept that. I have no sense of god; I'm the one at the centre of the universe and everything has meaning only in relation to me.'

The diary is always a dialogue between Luciana 1 and Luciana 2, a space I have created for myself so that there is a distance between the things I do and a supposedly higher being who judges those things without identifying with them. It is a pastiche stuffed with hurried reading, a melange to get me out of the tangled relationship between soul and body, helping to keep me away from any religious temptation. It is also a tremendously arrogant circle of self-reference.

Every so often, however, I do not manage to control reality and history: I don't know how to fit them into my schema. This always happens when my thoughts turn obsessively to the atom bomb.

'I can't explain things to myself – music painting poetry philosophy religion and nature mankind life death – when I think of the atom bomb. Its destructive power does not lie in the 300,000 Japanese it slaughtered, but rather in the sudden pulverization of all thought within us. If I think of the bomb, I think that nothing exists either inside or outside me.'

3 APRIL 1946

At the architecture faculty for Brandi's single lecture on art, which we are fortunately able to attend although we are not enrolled there.

In the PCI they keep talking about art, and artists keep talking about the PCI. Everyone is caught up in the relationship between art and class struggle. Picasso is the most controversial: he's a Communist but his art is not realist. And actually he doesn't even seem to concern himself with the class struggle. Someone vindicates him by saying that he is authentically Spanish, but that doesn't really seem to me an explanation. Guttuso says the same and indeed he doesn't disagree with Cubism, although he places everything in the context of so-called neorealist researches.

Political vanguardism and artistic vanguardism mingle with each other, as do cultural and class hostility to the bourgeoisie. Perhaps all this discussing is because everyone has a desire for novelty and the PCI is new to everyone. I too have a desire for novelty, but the Resistance is missing for me, whereas it was a great stimulus for painters. It aroused a desire for reality, a desire to paint history; it was an experience as powerful as a slap in the face. They became neorealists because they hadn't seen reality before and they added the 'neo' on account of the passion and curiosity with which they discovered the French avant-gardes. They have a horror of art for art's sake, or of artists who live through a tragic era but do not concern themselves with it.

15 APRIL 1946

'I'm happy to be alive and debating, happy with nature, happy to be discovering the particularity of myself and others, to be seeing the world and expressing what I experience, to be painting. I am happy with everything. The world is mine and I want everything.'

My happiness explodes on every third or fourth page of the diary. I must have been truly happy.

27 APRIL 1946

'At a meeting at the Brancaccio Theatre, the DC [Christian Democracy] party announced that it will support the Republic at the next referendum. The defeat of the monarchy therefore looks certain.

'There have been local government elections in many communes and the People's Bloc of Communists and Socialists won a very large number of them. These Communists seem really popular, even more than the Nenni Socialists.'

I make it known that I support the Republic: I find the monarchists ridiculous, even though that is what nearly all my childhood friends are. As for the parties, I write that if I could vote I wouldn't know which one to choose: not the DC, of course, but not even the PCI, because it is not liberal and if anything I would be in favour of a liberal Communism. But I'm not Socialist either, because of 'that wretch Nenni' (this is what I write) and 'because the Saragat variant is too right-wing'.

4 MAY 1946

Second Congress of Roman University Students. I don't understand what they're doing and what they want, but it must be interesting to sit all together there debating. Corbino, who I think is interior minister and should have made a contribution enabling all the delegates to take part in the forthcoming National Congress, said that he won't give one lira 'to pay for student balls'.

8 MAY 1946

Peace was sealed just a year ago. A year of peace has passed in Europe and the world. Yet a ferment lies beneath the surface that will inevitably find an outlet in one thing or another: A new war? A revolution?

16 MAY 1946

How Green Was My Valley. The film made a big impression on me: it tells of miners, poverty, unemployment and emigration. But I couldn't have drawn many political conclusions from it, because in my opinion it showed that 'all forms of government are the same if there's extreme poverty in the country. Prosperity is what really counts, and that certainly doesn't depend on the form of government.' Ergo: politics is pointless.

Fortunately, the monarchy makes me laugh. In the evening I write: 'I went to see the demonstration at the Quirinale, where the whole Savoy family – Umberto, Maria José, four children, even the nursemaid – appeared on the balcony.'

4 JUNE 1946

'It's two years since Rome was liberated. What have I learned? Almost nothing. My ideas are more confused than ever', I conclude despondently. Rather than politics, what really intrigues me is the nature of the world, the purpose and the cause of life.

I often think of the atom bomb, but always in relation to myself. Is it better to die alone or with the rest of mankind?

5 JUNE 1946

The Republic has triumphed, but the monarchists picked up a lot of votes.

11 JUNE 1946

A big festival for the Republican victory. Procession along the Corso and Via Nazionale. Romita,* De Gasperi,† Nenni and Togliatti speak at the Viminale Palace.

JUNE 1946

In the diary, I dwell for page after page on questions of morality, seriousness and responsibility, arguing that I should repress my emergent sexual instincts, which, to my disappointment, I discover not to be associated with love. The latter is not there, even if I try to invent it and eventually feel it for someone geographically distant, so that I won't have any actual problems of choice or behaviour to solve.

21 JUNE 1946

I see a Van Gogh for the first time, at Palazzo Venezia. Also a Monet and a Cézanne, an Utrillo and a Chagall. I am excited but in despair, because when I paint I end up imitating the last painters I have seen. I'm a prisoner of Modigliani, and Chagall leads me to make liberal use of black. But there's no spirit in my paintings:

---

* Giuseppe Romita: Socialist interior minister at the time.

† Alcide De Gasperi: founder of Christian Democracy and prime minister from 1945 to 1953.

they are frivolous. I realize that I am not an artist. But I continue to paint a lot.

2 JULY 1946

They've dropped another bomb, but only as a test, of course. On Bikini. They called it Gilda, on account of Rita Hayworth, a famous American actress. But they're all disappointed: the island didn't disappear into the sea as they had expected, nor did the waves engulf the seventy-five boats they'd moored there as guinea-pigs for destruction. They'd hoped to demonstrate that the weapon is ultra-effective. I am speechless.

A Soviet among the international observers invited to witness the experiment – from a distance – appears to have said, 'Is that all? It's no big deal.' Does he mean they're thinking of making something better?

9 AUGUST 1946

I turn seventeen. In Paris, a conference is underway to draw up the peace treaty and therefore to decide the fate of Trieste. But that doesn't matter to me much anymore. I'm in Venice and having fun.

20 AUGUST 1946: CORTINA

'I'm in Cortina: my wonderful parents treated me to this holiday at Villa Antica, a kind of summer boarding-school run by the gymnastics college on Via Po, under Prof. Fasulo. It's the first holiday I've had really on my own.'

I have great fun because I can do whatever I fancy. I go off to climb the Marmolada (there's not yet a cable car), scaling the vertical walls of the Contrin en route with rope and pitons. In the evening we go dancing at the Cristallino club. My early political appetites disappear, swallowed by mindless flirtations.

SEPTEMBER 1946: CALABRIA

I've never been in the South of Italy. Only once did I go for half a day to Naples, in early '46, to welcome a close friend of Papa's who was returning from America on board one of the first civilian steamships to come back into service across the Atlantic; I remember being struck by the almost deserted quay, still with very little traffic; the great size of the ship; and the US marines in full occupation of the port. But I've never seen the real South, beyond the metropolitan area of Naples.

My chance comes in September '46, late in the summer holidays before my last year of *liceo*, when I am invited by my friend Annuska Larussa – who, despite her name and surname, is of pure Calabrian blood on both her mother's and father's side.

Don Micco, her father, has not yet become what he will be for decades: the DC deputy for Catanzaro. But he is already a regional potentate – a count with a city *palazzo*, a landowner and an agrarian lawyer who has moved from Rome and established himself in the local high society.

His wife, who is in the course of separating from him, is quite different. Having grown up in Milan, she is more sophisticated and cannot bear her husband's heavy Calabrian manners.

More different still are Annuska and her sister Ismene, two girls much-courted in fashionable Roman society and always followed around by their English governess, Miss Molly. They are pupils at the legendary Cabrini religious college (in Via Aldovrandi, right opposite our house), where Mother once threatened to send me as a punishment, with the idea that it would remove me from the rebellious temptations of the secular Tasso.

But Annuska, my bosom friend, was different in a special way of her own: she didn't fit into any given context, dreamed of an ideal, romanticized Northern Europe, and finally married a Swede who they originally told her was the hero of Kon-Tiki, but in reality was his country's greatest theatre actor, Ulf Palme, a virtual homonym of his statesman cousin. She went to live with him in a snow-covered birch forest, not far from Stockholm.

So, I first encountered the South at the Larussas – not the Catanzaro *palazzo*, where only distant relatives now lived, but a more modest country house at Santa Maria, between the city and Copanello sea coast.

For me the South was 'Lower Italy': that was what we used to call it, reckoning that we from the North were looking at it from the top down. (Until my mother – an intelligent and open-minded woman – died at a hundred and one, I never managed to root out this expression from her mind.)

'I seem to have landed in a different country,' I wrote on arriving in the terra incognita. 'The countryside doesn't look at all like the only one I know well: the Veneto. Not only is nature harsher: yellow more than green, olives instead of grapes, prickly pears instead of orchards, houses clustered above one another on hilltops instead of distributed in the ordinary manner, vast empty spaces. Also the people speak an obscure language, the women are dressed in black and red (a costume that people here call *pacchiano*), and the men are ever on horseback, all *cutieddu*, a sword within reach to take action out of revenge or jealousy.'

On my first day there, I record with horror a spectacle that defies belief: 'A white sheet stained with blood in a window of a house in Santa Maria, proving the spouse's virginity on the day after a wedding.'

Men we come across remove their cap and bow, making me feel embarrassed for the first time because of my class.

It is 1946: farm labourers are already fighting for land and there are fierce clashes with landowners and their bailiffs. Yet I see and notice nothing but that affected servility. It does not occur to me that lurking within it is the rebelliousness that will accompany the epic of the land reform (the subject of my diploma thesis six years later).

I returned to Santa Maria for nearly two months in late 1950, to recover from concussion caused when I was riding my first Vespa and hit my head against the side of a bus. It was then that I really discovered the South – partly because in the meantime I had joined the PCI and begun to use my eyes.

Annuska's mother lived there all year round, waiting for her marriage annulment, and to liven up my convalescence she took me round the whole region in her tiny Fiat 500: from Reggio to Crotone, where bare moonlike mountains, dried white after the deforestation of previous centuries, surround the old Greek city. They were the lands of her friends, who had re-baptized themselves *trecentisti*, in sardonic reference to the agrarian reform that had deprived them of estates with more than 300 uncultivated hectares. They rarely came to stay at their houses in the area; the only one I remember, precisely because he spent quite a lot of time there, was Vittorio de Seta, who later, as an exile from his class, became the most thorough cinematic narrator of the Mezzogiorno.

My main discoveries of Calabria, however, during those two months of 1950, were made on the back of horses that my hosts kept in stables beside their house. Riding for whole days through uninhabited fields, I would only occasionally come across another solitary horseman, rifle slung over his shoulder – a hunter or a bandleader on his way to a procession.

In the country closest to Santa Maria, I met women stooped for hours gathering olives beneath the trees. They wore the traditional costume of Calabria: a bright red skirt and a black apron rolled at the waist. Since I hadn't yet given up my painter's trade, I returned from the region with many paintings of labourers and olive groves; my only artistic production ever would be from that time in Calabria.

In Catanzaro – which I remember being very cold that autumn – the PCI regional secretary was Gianni Di Stefano, a Roman sent there by headquarters whom I had met previously at Party meetings in the capital. He lived the tough life of full-timers at the front line, most of them from Emilia (the 'red reserve'), surviving on a pittance that was itself never sure to come through, in a very different society that they had to win over at a human level before they could do so politically. Also in the South, like Gianni, were many girls from Reggio or Modena working as sharecroppers, courageous pioneers of emancipation who often eventually married the Southerners they had gone there to 'colonize' in the name of communism, broken in (though never completely) to the ways and customs of the South.

Gianni took me along to some of his meetings, making me enter the steep alleyways of the villages winding up behind the sea. Here ancestors had once taken refuge from Saracens and malaria, and now, as men and women with mules descended at daybreak to cultivate some last clods of earth in the valley below, every storm caused more and more of the paths to fall away.

In those freezing branch meetings, barely heated by a brazier, I learned that in the previous years – when I, in my ignorance, had been holidaying in Santa Maria di Catanzaro – a veritable civil war had raged in the South. A war for land. And I also learned the names of the martyrs gunned down at Melissa and Montescaglioso, and heard for the first time of the armed confrontations at Andria and Corato.

Not many months later, in a hot, sultry July, I found myself once more in Santa Maria. This time I was on my first important political mission from the Communist Youth Federation (FGCI): to reunite its fragile university branches in the South.

After Bari, where I was solidly supported by the FGCI regional secretary, Giuseppe Cannata (the future mayor of Taranto), my next destinations were Messina and Catania.

I had never seen Sicily before, and I discovered what was different about it as soon as I arrived in the city across the straits. Two very shy comrades from the university picked me up at the station and accompanied me to a hotel, informing me that they would come the next morning to take me to the meeting. But the heat in the tiny, shabby room was so unbearable that I decided to go out (it was already past ten at night) and sit for a while in a café on the still-crowded main street. I sat down and began to spread out my notes for the next day's meeting at the university. Soon the two comrades came up and said in a low voice: 'We're sorry: don't worry about us, just go on with your work. But we must sit with you, because here a woman can't sit alone at a café.'

The next day, after the meeting, one of them took me to his place for lunch, but he did not sit at the table with his mother, his sister and me. 'It's embarrassing for a man to eat with a woman he doesn't know', they explained.

The train had taken fourteen hours to cover the arc of the Ionian Sea from Bari to Messina. And at Santa Maria Scalo my aristocratic friend Beatrice, who that winter had put me up and driven me round Calabria, appeared at my window in third class and handed me a thermos with fresh almond milk – a priceless gift on that hot and desolate journey. I had told her in advance of my movements. In those days, travelling in the South was like going to the Far West.

NOVEMBER 1946: MOTHER FINDS WORK

A great novelty: Mother has got a job. It's a little special, halfway between a business and social life; she does it from home, mainly over the telephone, with a couple of friends as partners and other friends and acquaintances as her 'network'. They find houses to let or sell. And since embassies and senior diplomats are returning to Rome, there is a lot of work to be had tracking down offices and residences for them. Thanks to my mother's almost pathological sociability, a mass of new foreign friends begin to troop through our house. Mother is in a state of great excitement. The only time she's worked before was for a month in the early Thirties, when she was somehow taken on to help organize Italy's participation in the Leipzig Fair of Small and Medium-Sized Industry. The task fired her with enthusiasm, but it had no lasting consequences. In those days, activity outside the home was not thought becoming for a lady, unless she was highly skilled in some field.

Now she is happy and fulfilled. Nino looks at her with the satisfaction that children show to each other when they invent a new game. But it is a serious matter: in fact, it is vital for the household economy during these years. She is proud to have become indispensable and autonomous, no longer dependent on her husbands.

Today I still wonder why she didn't rebel earlier but waited until the end of the Second World War to pluck up the courage for something as simple as a job – especially as it was necessary in view of our straitened circumstances. Until Mother remarried, there was no breadwinner in the family and we lived only on Father's allowance: a generous sum but never enough to see us through the month. (Mother constantly complained about it, blaming herself that she 'spent too much'.) But what kind of world was it, I ask myself, if even a woman as lively, curious and nonconformist as my mother did not rebel against such a humiliating condition?

On the other hand, that's what Mother was like, combining a desperate desire for order (partly due, perhaps, to the unsettled life that Grandfather had inflicted on the family) with a great open-mindedness also rooted in her childhood and adolescence. Though pleased to be working, she continued to feel guilty – now because she was no longer 'a good little wife always on call for her hubby'. She worriedly made us read and re-read the character profile that emerged from her answers to a psychological test in a fashionable French book of the time: *Voilà qui vous êtes*. It said: '*Pauvre madame!* Never try to combine the role of housewife with that of businesswoman: it would be a disaster.'

The discovery of these weaknesses irritated me and added to the incomprehension that set me against all the members of my family. My mother didn't like the company I kept and was afraid I might be exposed to sexual advances, so she saddled me with a Mary Poppins lookalike, a French chaperone by the name of Mademoiselle de la Forestière, who followed me around every afternoon. I felt ashamed with my comrades from Il Tasso, as if I were some kind of thief, but she didn't conceal that she found the bourgeoisie insufferable and eventually allowed me to find my way alone in the world.

I can't make out Mademoiselle de la Forestière, any more than I could in 1946! Fixed in my memory is an image of her trudging behind me on a balustraded staircase alongside the quadrangle of an INPS [social security] *palazzo*, in the vicinity of Piazza Quadrata. She had stubbornly refused to leave me on my own and was breathlessly following my every step, her hat slightly askew, her look filled with reproach, in the rear of thirty or more young classmates of mine, both male and female. In fact, I was engaging for the first time in a practice that had spread amid the postwar euphoria – the practice of 'gate-crashing' a party to which you hadn't been invited. It was a horrible thing to do, when I think about it: it meant that flocks of thoughtless youngsters crowded into apartments incapable of holding them all and often caused considerable damage. This was all the more distressing for families that had been thoughtful enough to donate the premises for their children's get-together, never imagining the barbarous mores that had been developing in recent years.

That gate-crashing was the first time I stepped out of line. On the other hand, my sense of shame with my new schoolmates over the presence of Mary Poppins was such that I stopped showing my face for a while.

Fortunately I became free of Mademoiselle in 1947, but I still can't understand how Mother managed to foist her onto me. Of course it allowed me to learn French, while inflicting in return a boundless sense of humiliation. It was rather like at primary school, where my classmates used to laugh at me because she made me wear gaiters: yes, beige or white gaiters, a rare and highly distinctive garment fashionable in Central Europe.

This respectability, in line with the canons of 'good families', seemed all the more bizarre in that Mother was not 'respectable' in the bourgeois sense of the word: divorced and remarried, with my grandparents' bohemian lifestyle behind her, she found social conventions stifling and derisory. That's how she was: constantly torn between libertarian, anti-bourgeois inclinations and a fear of not managing to be 'normal'.

Only much later, in old age, did Mother feel safe and free at last. And she was extraordinarily up-to-date: she lived to be a hundred and one, and my friends soon became hers almost more than mine. More than 200 came to offer their best wishes at her centenary.

On re-reading my diary pages for that period, I feel regretful about many things. My judgments about her were ungenerous, especially since I myself had difficulty becoming really free. In 1945–46, those who had not participated directly in the Resistance did not break immediately with their past: the old world clung on, albeit without any hope that it would last.

Everything came swiftly to a head in '47, when the world changed together with my family life. Mother progressed from casual house-hunter to settled estate agent, and I ventured once and for all beyond the confines of the Parioli ghetto. No one at home opposed admitting a diverse fauna of friends who swept away rules, habits and social distinctions.

FATHER

Father was very different. The youngest of eleven brothers and sisters, he had seen his mother die in childbirth in 1893, while his own father, Alfio (I saw him only in a photo, in a colonel's uniform), was a career soldier ever on the move from one city to another, so that his progeny, left to their own devices, took the opportunity to stay away from school. They were brought up mainly in a petty-bourgeois milieu in Milan, which, as I understood it, was secular and had socialist tendencies.

I never knew them, the Castellinas, because they were not very keen on Mother; she was unlike them in so many ways and doubtless reciprocated their mistrust. So, whereas Father remained very attached to the Liebmans – he went to see Grandmother and always had a warm relationship with Mother and her husband Nino – I had difficulty working out who and how many the Castellinas were. I saw very little of them, as did Father for that matter.

In the end I met a representative duo of Castellinas in the 1980s. I had been speaking at a festival of the Party of Proletarian Unity (PdUP) in a Milan park, and an old lady came up to me in the company of a younger woman. 'I am Aunt Ines and this is your cousin Adriana', she said. 'We saw your name, which is the same as ours, on the festival posters, so we thought we'd come and meet you.'

After that I saw quite a lot of them. Aunt Ines was already in her nineties but looked the spitting image of me: high cheek-bones, large space between nose and mouth, just like Father too. She, in particular, soon won me over. Unmarried, but certainly no virgin, she had just acquired a free travel pass and spent much of her time discovering the streets of Milan and things she had never seen before.

So, at the age of fifty-five, I came to realize that there was a lot of Castellina as well as Liebman in me: and that I was perhaps more Milanese than Triestine after all.

Peace

26 SEPTEMBER 1946

Count Sforza, the little old man who lives at the end of our Via Vallisneri, a few houses further up, has become chairman of the Consulta – *a committee that is supposed to lay the ground for an Assembly charged with preparing a new Constitution. Nino says that many of the people in it were in prison. In all, he said, they served 433 years. I didn't think the Fascists had put so many people in jail.*

A majority of them seem to be Communists.

10 OCTOBER 1946

The schools are reopening. I'll be in the third year of liceo. *I'm exempt from school fees because Father is a disabled war veteran and has been decorated with the* Croce di Guerra: *he has a hole in his back where a bullet hit him at Caporetto.*

25 OCTOBER 1946

At last! A major exhibition of contemporary French painting at the Modern Art Gallery. There are the Cubists, Picasso and Braque, as well as Matisse. They are anti-bourgeois, not in the sense Mother means, but because they scoff at the triviality of those who think that the world has only one dimension, a single possible interpretation. They really intrigue me.

10 NOVEMBER 1946

At the Galleria Margherita on Via Bissolati, I saw for the first time a large collection of paintings by Renato Guttuoso, the Sicilian painter in the PCI. One series is called Gott mit uns, *many of them from before the end of the war. They are very beautiful and relate a lot of our recent history.*

I was struck by a sentence of Tristan Tzara's that I read: 'To the bourgeoisie that says individual, communism has replied man.'

Today there is voting in Rome for the city council. My people are voting for the People's Bloc, but they're not all that convinced. They chose it because there are Socialists on the list, but they can't take the fact that there are also Communists.

17 NOVEMBER 1946

Another International Students' Day. I saw a few of the people from Il Tasso. The ones in the PCI talked about the International Philosophy Congress that is taking place during these days. They're very excited about this new thing that's appeared: existentialism. They have their doubts about it but are curious, because it's a philosophy of crisis, but also of the bourgeoisie's bad conscience over the rootlessness of its existence. But they're pleased because it's the first time that Marxism has taken its place among philosophers as of right.

I know nothing about either Marxism or existentialism. I ought to read, but I don't know where to begin.

7 DECEMBER 1946

A very fine film at the Capranica: Casablanca.

13 JANUARY 1947

Saragat walked out of the Congress of the PSIUP, which is apparently what the Socialists have officially been calling themselves. Two parties are being created: the PSI, with Nenni, and the PSDI with Saragat. Nino is very pleased. I'm a lot more undecided, since, as time goes by, this Nenni no longer seems to me a 'wretch', as I hastily assumed he was after the Liberation. Besides, now that I know the Communists a little, they don't seem so bad. I spend more and more time with them at Il Tasso, because they are the most intelligent and I'm beginning to have rather more fun with them than with my traditional friends.

24 FEBRUARY 1947

My Communist schoolmates took me to the Youth Front, which also includes the Socialists.

We were there with guys from other schools, south of the Parco del Celio, where the Front has some offices. The leader is a certain Enrico Berlinguer. I know who he is because he's the son of the epuratore* *from Sassari who's friends with Nino and once came to dinner with his other son, Giovanni. He's even less sociable and more serious than his brother. The first day he asked us – timidly, it is true – to move some benches for him.*

6 MARCH 1947

In my diary I report that I am 'working' for the Front, but I don't specify what my new political activity consists of – apart from shifting benches. On the other hand, I'm much taken with my new friendships: 'through them', I write, 'I come directly into contact with the problems of all kinds of people, and with many ideas that

---

* *Epuratore*: member of one of the commissions responsible for purging the civil service after the end of Fascism.

broaden my own thinking. I have realized that a whole mass of people, including so many of my traditional friends, live as if it were twenty years ago, outside time, thereby displaying something more than stupidity or lack of awareness. They don't realize how important the social question is right now, or that bourgeois conventions and principles must be abolished. I don't know how to explain my thoughts on these things, but I can see that I too am in the midst of a social crisis.'

12 MARCH 1947

'The social crisis remains acute. On my desk there are now piles of books on politics, economics and history. The people at the Front have asked me to join a group dealing with the reform of history teaching, which needed to be freed of "Crocean canons".'*

I don't know much about these 'Crocean canons', but I am convinced that history needs to be treated in a new way. 'It is disgraceful,' I write, 'that schools continue to teach on the basis of the Crocean canons, speaking of the Risorgimento in schemas laid down by the past monarchical regime for which the whole thing was a glorification of the House of Savoy. What should be emphasized is the role of the workers' movement, the influence of Marxism.'

In section 'C' at the Tasso *liceo*, where I was studying, the teacher of Italian, history and philosophy was Giuseppe Petronio, a short, ugly man, very arrogant and quite extraordinary. It is to him that I owe nearly everything I came to understand: that is, that I had misunderstood everything and needed to subject my thinking to a

---

* That is, the idealist philosophy of history associated with Benedetto Croce.

complete overhaul. He sorted out the tangle in which my scant and hasty learning had become caught up. He was the first to give a meaningful answer to the rush of my unanswered questions, the first to offer me some keys.

Petronio treated me brusquely and liked to take the mickey out of me: 'So, what does *Onorevole* Castellina make of this?' It is true, though, that the business of the Crocean canons and my induction into the Youth Front tended to make me sound off about things.

'They say Petronio is a Socialist,' I write, 'and also that he's head-over-heels in love with a fellow party member, the young and stunningly beautiful art history teacher Tullia Romagnoli Carrettoni' (who would be my colleague in the European Parliament forty years later).

It was thanks to them that, having studied whole nights long, as well as whole days on the wonderful, austere benches of the old National Library (then still at the Collegio Romano), I came away with a bizarre score from my school-leaving exam at the *liceo*: six (the minimum pass grade) in every subject except history, philosophy and art. In those I got two nines and a ten.

I also got six in Italian, although to write it would become my trade in later years. The reason for this poor mark was that I got bogged down in an essay on a theme that proved to be difficult and confused – and which, looking back, was actually misconceived. We were asked to express our views on the concepts of nation and nationalism, but the framework seemed to me to attach too much weight to mythology. Caught up as I was in battling the famous Crocean canons, all that mattered for me were economic interests: the material forces that make real history. So I wrote at length about Belgium and Holland, using them as an example of regions carved up and recombined into two countries to suit the divergent business strategies (one industrial, the other commercial) of their respective bourgeoisies. Any other factors were idle chatter. (Today, when I see Walloons and Flemish arguing even about such things as the limits of their cemeteries, I feel ashamed that I so crudely dismissed communities which, though imagined, do not interest themselves exclusively in steelmaking or transport.)

The preparations for my school-leaving exam were a wonderful period. Despite the effort, I managed to write a few lines in my diary recording the emotion with which I read in every field, sometimes well outside the school curriculum. At the National Library I found all the books I wanted and fell in love with Plotinus; he seemed to offer a systematization of the philosophical schema I had constructed to bring my own life into order. Over the years, I had dreamed up a dualism (and a dialogue) between what my diary called Luciana 1 and Luciana 2: that is, between my subjective ego and the objective events and characters of the real world, into which Luciana 2 was invited as an aloof observer. Now, however, I came to realize that I was in the very midst of that world, that my essence was not something other than what I did but included it. My inner self served for understanding the objects and events of external experience, through the impressions offered by the senses.

I drew the conclusion (which I used to justify my activism) that the more one does, the more one lives and the more one's inner self is enriched.

In the evenings, with the doors of the Collegio Romano about to close, the notes of organ concertos played by Germani began to waft through the windows from the nearby church of Sant'Ignazio. It became a place to linger for a while, before returning home for more study.

Peace

In those days, people went a lot to concerts. My diary is always mentioning them, especially those at the Teatro Adriano (now a multiplex cinema), where we would enter apprehensively to see the fascinating maestro Franco Ferrara. He was a pallid figure, sometimes on the point of collapse after the first few bars of music, and in the end he caused us great sorrow when he had to give up conducting.

30 MARCH 1947

Antonio Giolitti – a Communist and son of a pre-Fascist prime minister – is back from a trip to Yugoslavia at the head of a Youth Front delegation. At the offices in Celio it is said that Tito received them in his partisan's uniform and offered them chocolates, vermouth and cigarettes. Young volunteers are building a railway there, and it's possible that brigades will be organized in Italy to go and help them. I'd really like to go and see this Yugoslavia for myself.

3 APRIL 1947

At the Constituent Assembly they are discussing a lot of things to which I've never given any thought – even illegitimate children and the question of divorce, which someone said already exists in reality, but only for the rich. Although my parents weren't rich, I know how much money they had to pay to obtain an annulment from the Sacra Rota.

I'd never thought that family matters were political.

4 APRIL 1947: LA GARBATELLA

I was in La Garbatella, the quarter I read about so often in Il Messagero *during the occupation because, along with San Lorenzo, it was one of the most heavily bombed on account of the rail yards at Tiburtino and Ostense. I went there for a meeting of the Front, the first on the outskirts that I've been invited to attend. It was quite a discovery: older people were there too and they said that some residents of the area, including women, were already conspiring against Fascism in the Thirties and later kindled the armed resistance after 8 September. Only the survivors were there: large numbers were shot or died in German camps, where they were deported after their arrest. Terrible stories, all of parents with many children, generally very poor and courageous workers or artisans. I felt ashamed thinking of the passivity of people in my parts of the city who called themselves anti-Fascists.*

At the Youth Front meeting, Orlando Lombardi also spoke about these things: he's still quite young (little over twenty) and works at Ottica Meccanica Italia. He said that, during the occupation, one of the things he did was go to the University with the underground military group of La Garbatella; they were called there by Trombadori, head of GAP, the Roman urban partisans, to free students who had been calling for a demonstration and, when surrounded by the Germans, had exchanged gunfire with them in an attempt to escape.

On the night the Allies arrived, 3–4 June two years ago, Orlando went gun-in-hand with his brother and an older man called Natalini (who's now the PCI branch secretary) to occupy the Fascist headquarters in La Garbatella – the 'Villetta' [Little Villa], so called because that is what it looks like, and the very building on a hill where we were today. It subsequently became the local PCI headquarters, named after one of the many killed in the area, Giuseppe Cinelli, who was shot at the Fosse Ardeatine.

The memorial stone for Cinelli is still there, and the Villetta remains a legendary meeting place for the left in Rome – one of the few PCI branch offices spared during these years, still functioning but with a history all its own. When the Party dissolved in 1991, the same Orlando Lombardi refused to accept that his place was in what became the PDS after the Rimini Congress. As he had done on that night in '44 – in more dramatic circumstances, to be sure – Orlando and a number of other comrades occupied the Villetta for a second time, so as not to lose what they claimed to be their house. Since a majority of PCI members in La Garbatella had opted to join Rifondazione Comunista, the historical headquarters was thus divided between the two successor organizations: one on the first floor, the other on the second. More recently, however, a majority of members of the local Rifondazione branch left the Party and joined Sinistra Ecologia e Libertà, together with a majority of the local branch of the PDS, who did not want to enter the newly formed Partito Democratico. In a way, after twenty years, La Garbatella has thus become united again. Orlando would be happy with this: but he died in 1995.

10 APRIL 1947

Another place on the outskirts, for another meeting of the Front. This time at Tiburtino III. It's a different Rome, even further out than La Garbatella and more recent, with hovels worse than the 'Alberghi', those strangely named blocks now falling to pieces in the area behind Ostiense, where pilgrims were meant to stay in the Holy Year 1925, no less, but*

---

* *Albergo*, though also a poetic term for 'abode' generally, is mainly used with the meaning of 'hotel'.

were chased out by people evicted from gutted popular districts: one huge red building and a white one, which, I was told, became 'subversive' (i.e. anti-Fascist) dens from Day One. Here in Tiburtino the poverty is more overt, because the old residents have been joined by evacuees from the countryside around Rome through which the front line passed – even by people from as far away as La Ciociaria. There were also some local kids at our meeting: so different from us (who were mainly students) that we felt embarrassed.

The suburbs put an end to my innocence; I discovered a sense of guilt on account of my privileges.

14 APRIL 1947

'The teachers are on strike. I didn't know they would be striking too.'

So many new things are assailing me. My life has changed. I discover with pleasure that I've hardly been concerned with myself this last year, but rather with the things and people with whom I come into contact. I write that life is fantastic.

At school I see and debate a lot with Ageo Savioli (future theatre critic for *L'Unità*), and with the Bertelli brothers, my real mentors on my road to the PCI: Sergio (later a historian, now on the extreme Right); Carlo, then very caustic towards me, whether because of my social–cultural distance from the PCI or because of my naive enthusiasms. (He became a refined lecturer in modern art and director of the Brera museum in Milan; I met him recently, and he helped me see many things at the Milan Triennale that I would never have perceived with my own eyes.)

A new, very different guy arrives from Turin: he's not interested in painting or architecture or even history, but only in medicine. His name is Marcel Hutter and he has a Russian mother who's a dancer and the semi-wife of a well-known anti-Fascist: Aldo Garosci. I learn from him a few things about the Partito d'Azione people. And I listen to him talk about super-industrial Turin, a city I don't know at all, where there are so many workers who fought in the Resistance.

3. DISCOVERY OF THE WORLD

Now that the world has become global and France is a little country more or less on the margins, I don't know whether it is possible to understand what Paris represented for my generation and a dozen previous ones. After the Second World War it meant even more than it had in the past, because of the years of abstinence imposed on us by Fascism and the war.

The rest of the world scarcely existed: we didn't know how it was constructed, and so we had little curiosity about it. Paris, on the other hand, was everything we knew to exist in the world but had hitherto been denied: books, theatre, cinema and especially, in my case, painting. Of course it was also unrestricted freedom, the only modernity we could succeed in imagining. America had not yet arrived.

So, when I heard at the Youth Front that a student exchange between Rome and Paris was being organized for Easter, I saw to it that I was included in the group, even though the trip was intended for university students and I was still in the third year of *liceo*.

In April 1947, individual passports were still being granted only in special cases. Some eighty of us were therefore issued with a collective document and took a train that was supposed to reach Paris in forty-eight hours. My emotion was such that my diary has only one laconic phrase about our departure: 'I've done it!'

There were quite a lot of young painters in our group – Dorazio, Vespignani, Muccini, Guerrini, Perilli, Carla Accardi, Busiri, Aymonino, and others less well known. This Youth Front trip was their first opportunity to go and see the longed-for Impressionists, the Cubists, and the galleries that had made Paris one with modern painting.

During the train journey, they organized a preview showing of their own works, and for me it was a memorable initiation.

I have a photo of our group at Bardonecchia on the border with France, our faces radiant with expectation, the journey a fantastic prelude to adventure. To cross a frontier – for the first time – was a historic event: even the railwaymen were moved.

We pulled into the Gare de Lyon in the morning, after two sleepless days of talking and singing. Those waiting for us at the station were due to leave that evening to take our places back home in Rome. At this point Giovanni Berlinguer, our guide on behalf of the International Union of Students, realized that he had matched the numbers of Italians and French, but that no one had sorted out who was to stay where.

There was a moment of panic. But Giovanni stayed calm and, perched on the little wall in the square outside the station, he began to single out the Italians one by one and to ask the French crowded round him to take their pick. It was like at a horse fair: all that was missing was the showing of teeth.

I was worried where I might end up, so I settled on a clean and respectable-looking French girl and suggested we make a private arrangement: we'd choose each other and notify the organizers accordingly. For me this was a bad move – or perhaps, in the end, a real stroke of fortune.

I hadn't expected that Monique Giot would be quite so respectable. She led me through the caves leading to the Metro, and there I realized to my dismay that our destination was Charenton, right at the end of the line. Virtually no longer Paris. Last train at midnight.

At the exit, on the tiled walls of my first real Metro station, a number of black fists – a nineteenth-century design from the early days of advertising – had fingers pointing outward to Charbon Giot, the prosperous firm of wholesalers that belonged to my host's family. I soon had a chance to meet the family members and dependants – the latter wearing black cloth oversleeves – all seated at a long table laid for a feast. 'You see', Monique informed me, 'today is my parents' silver wedding anniversary.'

It was a hard blow to take. I had come to Paris to find the symbol of modernity and landed in this stage-setting. Even today, I jump if I see an advertisement with the fateful fist in some old newspaper, or if someone reminds me of those 'oversleeves'.

It took me many years to understand that there was also a *France profonde*, a reactionary, bigoted petty-bourgeoisie both urban and rural, which accounted for Vichy and so many other things in the country's history – a France not descended in a straight line from Robespierre, the Commune and the Popular Front, and for which Cubism or Jean-Paul Sartre was more alien than for us Italians.

But I was also excited about Paris, and my diary has a few hurried lines warning that I would not have much time to spare and would record my memories when I was back in Rome. Meanwhile, I could only cry out that all I had seen 'is enough for me to express irrepressible enthusiasm for a city that has opened up unsuspected horizons, where everyone does as they please, where you can feel alone in a crowd and at the same time experience everything the crowd can give you. What is more, the city is giving me back the assurance to paint; I understand that Paris is the source of a kind of artistic *prana*.'

I walked round the city following the itinerary I had learned from Severini's journal in *Il Mercurio*. The holy places of painting, the haunts of the artists: La Closerie des Lilas, Le Lapin agile, Le Moulin de la Galette …

Yet, in the city of wonders, although the Giots were kind to me (one evening, dressed to the nines, they took me to the Opéra), my relationship with them was not exactly easy. After a few days I stopped coming home at night. And a week into my stay, they were so alarmed that they decided to tell my mother that I was out all the time and they hardly ever saw me. What should they do? Meanwhile, in Rome, my mother was worried because Monique never left the house.

I didn't sleep in Charenton because in Paris the night is the most fascinating part of the day. I couldn't let it slip, once chance had landed me at the heart of the most famous season in Saint-Germain-des-Prés.

On one of my first few days in Paris, it so happened that I was seated on the banks of the Seine munching a sandwich, so that I would not have to return to the Giots for lunch, when I met a member of our group who, like all the others, was wandering through the city. He was Emanuele Lauricella, later to become the chief gynaecologist at the University of Rome, under whose care I would place myself for the birth of my two children. Emanuele's billeting experience had been the opposite of mine: being himself from a very respectable Catholic family, he had ended up in a house where – as he put it, shocked – the portrait of Pius XII was hanging in the loo but where permanent confusion reigned, weird people kept coming and going, and nothing seemed in order. 'Come and see for yourself', he suggested, 'no one will even notice.'

So, in my quest for lodgings closer to the centre, I made my way to 26, rue de Tournon in the middle of the *quartier* of *quartiers*. It was where the Simon family lived: father and mother, two children in addition to Emanuele's exchange partner, and a girl, Denise, who remained a great friend of mine even after she moved to New York when her husband, Luis Safir, was sent there by a French newspaper.

There was nothing ordinary about the Simon household: it was one of the centres of the cultural life of the period, a kind of annex of the Café de Flore, where all its lead players passed through: from Sartre to Simone de Beauvoir, from Queneau to Prévert. I had heard some of them mentioned before: for example, Visconti had staged a controversial production of Sartre's *Huis Clos* at the Teatro Eliseo in Rome, and I had also read *Le mur* (as always in *Il Mercurio*, which I bought for its section on the figurative arts). On the other hand, many of the others who got together at the tables of the Café de Flore became well known only many years later.

Not even Juliette Gréco's name was yet on everyone's lips: I heard her sing 'Barbara' at the launch of the Tabou, the most celebrated *cave* of the day, which would eventually make her famous. Sartre too spent many an evening there. For years I displayed as a trophy the club membership card that was given to me that spring.

Two more young unknowns were the aspiring filmmakers Roger Vadim and Christian Marquand. I and my friend Claudia (who had had the good luck to be assigned a place at Pigalle) once spent a whole night walking with them in the mysterious streets of Paris, away from the early postwar tourist circuits, before we ended up at dawn in the Russian Orthodox church where the future director of

Barbarella and husband of Brigitte Bardot and Jane Fonda took us to listen to the chants of that unfamiliar liturgy.

With some disappointment, Claudia and I remarked that these two young men of almost the same age as ourselves had not so much as touched us. Nor, for that matter, did the elder Simon brother – the strikingly handsome Jean-Jacques.

These young Frenchmen seemed indifferent to sex, blasé, as if it was an activity that could at best interest only backward Italians. The distinction between sex and eroticism was unknown to us; and we two girls, not bad-looking but ordinary, aroused no curiosity in boys who were not subjected to the abstinence of their Italian counterparts.

Many years later, I joked with Jane Fonda about my night with the man who later become her husband. That was in the early Seventies and I was accompanying Jane – who had meanwhile divorced Vadim – along the Californian coast to the suburbs of Los Angeles. She was due to speak there about Vietnam, filling theatres with good conservative Americans whom she tried to win over by telling them some of the tricks of Hollywood and the cinema, and stories of how the French director first transformed her from a kid girl into a sex symbol.

Politics too were discussed in the Simon home and the Café de Flore, to whose tables I was invited as a kind of folklore item. I was the *petite écolière italienne* who sometimes took heart and spoke of her native country, painting a grim picture of it as backward and impoverished in order to heighten the impact. They were all on the Left, of course, but it was a Left I had never encountered before – very different from the Circolo Tasso or the Youth Front or my friends at the architecture faculty, more easygoing, more rounda-bout. For them politics was mixed up with other things; they were also often difficult to understand, and not only because they spoke

French quickly and used expressions I had never read in a book. The fact is that in Italy I had never met any left-wing intellectuals: I had only heard their names and read some of their writings; I was too little to mix with them, my family circle too distant. It was in Paris that I first discovered this precious species that would later populate so much of my life – and so it seemed to me at first that it was a French speciality.

In Saint-Germain I also discovered the arrogance and self-centredness of intellectuals – something very French, in fact. They showed contempt for (almost) everything and were always elusive, like people who can afford anything and therefore no longer enjoy the diversity of what exists, beginning with women. It was the opposite of Italy, where everyone was hungry for everything because everything had been forbidden them.

Maison Simon, 26, rue de Tournon, 6ème arrondissement: this was a turning-point in my understanding of the world. As Guy Debord later wrote of this milieu: 'It was the place where everyone inside regarded everyone outside as irrelevant.'

24 APRIL 1947

The trip to Paris that the painters made with us resulted in a sharpening of the public dispute between figurative and abstract artists. What Dorazio, Perilli and Accardi saw there encouraged them to take up cudgels against those who claimed that only figurative artists could serve a social and political function. Together with the slightly older Turcato, they wrote shortly afterwards a manifesto with the polemical title 'Formalists and Marxists', while Guttuso and Treccani painted canvases depicting workers and landless squatters.

Togliatti furiously rounded on a show of abstract artists in Bologna. But then everyone got together again for a collective exhibition in Prague, in the framework of the first World Youth Festival that opened there in July.

I was confused. Similarly, many others who felt lost displayed incredible ingenuity in trying to catch up and fill the gaps. There was much talk of a 'rational' yet 'organic' architecture, especially from Scandinavia, and my architect friends dreamed of nothing more than going there to see it for themselves. Meanwhile they gave birth to their own collective studio, the Studio Architetti Progressisti.

On one thing, at least, everyone was in agreement: a loathing of the EUR district of southern Rome, which had not yet acquired its final 'R' and was still called EU, after the Esposizione Universale scheduled for 1942 but never held because of the war. Nowadays, to be frank, those blocks with Gruyère-like holes in them, designed by the architect Marcello Piacentini, do not seem to me so bad, but at the time they were thought to be the acme of Fascism. Toti Scialoja, malicious as ever, wrote that 'they stood waiting for their rightful residents, Hitler and Nero, to be seated on the Böcklinesque quadrille'.

25 APRIL 1947

Today I went to the Parco Nemorense, where a festival was being held to mark the second anniversary of the Liberation. There was a beauty contest for children, almost all of them ugly, and people danced to the music of the Stefer* band. Fausto Nitti gave a speech.†

---

* Società delle Tramvie e Ferrovie Elettriche di Roma: the now defunct tram company covering the Rome region.

† Francesco Fausto Nitti (1899–1974): a prominent opponent of the Fascist regime and postwar journalist.

26 APRIL 1947

I went to the Congress of University Students and I too can't wait to leave this wretched liceo. *I'm nearly always with these older guys on the Left. I have much more fun than before, even if with my old friends I used to go by car to Ostia instead of by train. Now we're also in the gods at the theatre.*

27 APRIL 1947

There is much talk of Antonio Gramsci, one of the founders of the PCI, because it is the anniversary of his death ten years ago, in a Rome clinic where he was admitted after spending a great deal of time in prison. They also commemorated him at the Constituent Assembly. It came as a big surprise to me that he's so important, since I'd heard his name only from Professor Sante Ciancarelli, a friend of Uncle Guido Liebman, who was a Fascist before the race laws and is a doctor like him. Thanks to this friendship, our whole family has always received treatment at the clinic that bears his name (Father had his stomach ulcer operated on there); Professor Ciancarelli opened it in Via Morgagni, having worked for many years at the Quisisana Hospital. It was there that he met Gramsci.

I asked Father and he confirmed this to me. But he too has only a rough idea of who this Gramsci was.

30 APRIL 1947

I met an arrogant but very handsome guy at the Youth Front, the editor of the magazine Pattuglia: *Gillo Pontecorvo. They say he was a very courageous* gappista *[urban partisan] in Milan. He returned of his own free will from France, where he had taken refuge as a Jew. (Not all Jews hid, then.) He questioned me drily about a host of things, making me feel*

139

ridiculous. He spoke badly of all American films. But I'd read that, in these very days, Charlie Chaplin and many like him in America had been indicted and persecuted for being Communists.

3 MAY 1947

Something terrible has happened in Sicily: they've killed a lot of peasants who gathered with their women and children on the plains of Portella della Ginestra, near Palermo, to celebrate the First of May. It seems that landowners' guards opened fire with automatic weapons from the hillside, to strike fear in the Left after weeks in which the People's Bloc had won in every province.

In Rome there was a protest march from the Basilica di Massenzio to Piazza Esedra, where we too went from the Front. Workers were also there, from Minzolini, as always, but also from other factories I hadn't heard of before: Fatme and Breda.

8 MAY 1947

At the University the students have decided to strike on Saturday, the 17th, to protest against the Rector's demand for a contribution of 4,000 lire. Not everyone agrees with the action: the FUCI, the organization of Catholic university students, has dissociated itself.

9 MAY 1947

I write that I'm angry because I've heard (on the radio?) that the sessions at the Montecitorio have rejected the draft Articles 30 and 31 for the Constitution. These call for economic planning and stipulate that political rights and nationality should be conferred only on those who work for a living. I would simply take away the citizenship of those who live on profits! My break with high Roman society, which works little or not at all, is now complete.

17 MAY 1947

Today, the day of the students' strike, we marched to the Ministry of Education, in Trastevere.

A pause in my obsessional preparations for the final liceo exam. Went to see Paisà. *Wonderful.*

23 MAY 1947

Yesterday, many of those I work with at the Front went to the first National Youth Conference of the PCI. They told me that Togliatti spoke a lot about the crisis facing young people, who no longer know how to dream and have lost confidence in themselves and the world.

25 MAY 1947

The first effects of my new associations are beginning to make themselves felt. I'm attracted to them, but at the same time I'm frustrated that they know so much more than I and are all deeply involved in the 'social question'. I know nothing and am a nobody. From my stratospheric self-assurance I fall into the belief that I am a failure. 'Until a short time ago', I write sorrowfully, 'I thought I was capable of doing what I wanted: painting, writing, anything. I had an absolutely subjective, self-referential conception of the intellect; I had never measured my brain against other people's. I used to be full of self-confidence; now, as soon as I'm given some responsibility,

I take fright that I will not be equal to it. I have neither brilliance nor quickness of mind. All I can do is fall back diligently on books. This year I have certainly learned many things and I'm richer in social and cultural experiences, but I'm light years away from the other comrades. I think I am more like I will be, but I will no longer be like I was or dreamed of being, like I thought I could always be.'

Evidently, my first engagement with the Communists had catastrophic effects: the first time I met them, in 1945 at the demonstration in Trieste, they gave me a beating; now they were destroying my ego. They were also thwarting my greatest ambition: to be free and independent. This, I now realized, was really very complicated, and in my enthusiasm for new ideas I ended up suppressing all longing for freedom for myself as something petty and mystifying. To enjoy it while others did not, or to have it without gauging where the freedom of others limited mine, seemed to me shameful. The assertion of my personal convictions over those of the collective seemed an individualist act, arrogant and petty bourgeois.

My rigidity on this point would be fervent and tenacious, so that when I joined the PCI I was for years the most disciplined of militants. Only in the late 1950s, after reading new things and meeting new people, did I loosen a little my anti-individualist orthodoxy. But since those earlier days a visceral antipathy for the ideology of the Radicals has always remained part of my character.

JULY 1947: PRAGUE

Although we were not yet at university (we had only just sat our school-leaving exams), my *liceo* benchmate Pucci Piccinato and I were exceptionally allowed to join the Italian delegation to the

Council of the International Union of Students, which was due to meet in Prague at the same time as the World Youth Festival.

When we arrived in the Czechoslovak capital, the great event was already under way. It was the first in a long series of annual occasions, each in an East European capital, which came to an end only with the collapse of the Soviet Union, although by then it had been beset with contradictions and disputes for some time.

The most famous of the festivals, after the launch in Czechoslovakia, was the one ten years later in Moscow. It was a magical moment for the Soviet Union, when it was opening up to the world and a new sense of freedom seemed to herald a turning-point that everyone expected but which never came. The city was invaded by tens of thousands of young people; there were popular dances at night inside the Kremlin walls, a stone's throw from Stalin's embalmed body, among the onion domes of the Orthodox churches that flanked the seat of Communist power; and the first jazz orchestras were appearing on socialist soil. From Italy came the Roman Jazz Band of Carletto Loffredo, who had begun his career immediately after the Liberation in a night club on Via Capo le Case. I was introduced to the new music by Antonio Gambino, later one of the founders of the daily *Repubblica*.

The Youth Festival in Prague was never surpassed, however, because in its way it marked the true end of the war (and of an era) – the explosion of joy of a new generation arriving from all continents and telling its stories in a Babel of tongues. Certain that freedom for everyone was just around the corner and guaranteed for all time, the Italians – nearly all leaders of the Left that has now taken its pension – were discovering politics; and love.

Forced to share the narrow spaces assigned to them, the two heads of the large Italian delegation could not have been more different from each other: Marisa Musu, a former GAP member from Rome, blunt and genial, already a very youthful candidate for the Central Committee of the PCI; and Mario Pirani, a full-timer for the Youth Front about to be transferred to its Venice branch (later to work as a journalist at *L'Unità* and, after leaving the Party, at the ENI state oil and gas monopoly and then at the daily *Repubblica*). Pirani was sarcastic almost to the point of iconoclasm. I remember being especially struck by the manicure set he placed on the mat by his folding bed – a bizarre object for the time and place.

Italo Calvino was there too – although I didn't yet know what Italo Calvino was, and neither did he. He had been sent from *L'Unità* in Turin. I read his festival reports only much later, in compilations held at the headquarters of the Rome University branch of the PCI. Someone must have realized the Turinese journalist was promising material.

The Cold War had already begun – Churchill's Fulton speech, introducing the term 'iron curtain' into the political lexicon, dated from a few months earlier – but we were not yet aware of it. In Greece the civil war was actually hot. But we knew little or nothing of that either. Only now, on looking back, does it occur to me that I didn't meet any Greeks that summer: the ones who might have attended the festival were 'in the mountains', embroiled in the first postwar guerrilla campaign.

Anti-Communism too was gathering momentum. But although the Communists had been driven out of the Western governments into which the tide of the Resistance had carried them, the hostility was not as visceral as it would become after 1948. Nor did the Soviets yet seem obsessed with fears of an attack by their former allies and the resulting need to ensure total control of their 'buffer zone'. Czechoslovakia was Communist, but still democratic.

Yet the festival was marked by an ugly sore that should have made us think: the delegation representing American youth associations, which had been expected until the last moment, failed to arrive; the most extremist wing of the US administration managed to block funding of their journey, on the grounds that the event was a sinister gathering of Communists.

We paid no heed to the clouds on the horizon. The aristocratic city that some of us knew from the works of Kafka was placed at our disposal: everything – museums, shows, concerts, transport, canteens – was open and free of charge. Only young people were to be seen in the streets or parks and along the river; any older folk were lost in the crowd.

Prague revealed itself to us as Zlatá Praha, the golden city, full of wonders and mystery. The welcome at the festival could not have been more marvellous, the political magic around the long, broad, ever-crowded Wenceslas Square compounded by the literary fascination of the narrow streets of Malá Strana.

I went back to Prague fifty years later, in 1996, curious to see the city again. But I went with some trepidation, since chance – though perhaps not only chance – had given the city a fundamental role in my life. There, in 1947, I discovered the world which for me coincided with Communism, in the sense that it seemed the only possible key for me to understand the new map of the world, so unlike the one I had known before. There I encountered the PCI for the first time in flesh and blood, with its relative prejudices; there I enrolled in the international brigade to help in building the Youth Railway in Yugoslavia; and there too, three years later, at the next Congress of the International Union of Students, I saw the delegation of Chinese students get off the train at the central station – air travel was still a rarity – all clad in military uniforms and fresh from the victorious battle against the army of Chiang Kai-Shek and its American backers under General Marshall. Two decades later Prague was once more at the centre of my life, when the city through which I had entered the PCI became the one because of which I was driven out. This would be the history of *Il Manifesto*, which began precisely with the Soviet invasion of Czechoslovakia in 1968.

I had not returned to Prague after those far-off days: first, because my expulsion from the PCI meant that the Husák regime would not have allowed me in, and then because I was afraid of wounding my memory of it. But in 1996 I was drawn into a visit when I was attending the film festival in Karlovy Vary – a town where more or less everything (Belle Époque hotels, fountains, thermal baths, cafés with little orchestras) had resisted the march of time, so that I felt not alienated but offended only by the block of cement, the Thermal, that 'actually existing socialism' had decided to build to the glory of the seventh art.

Gisy Weissman – the grand old man of Czech cinema who, cut off from his homeland by the black August of '68, was now returning with an American passport, half citizen, half tourist, his body resident in California but his heart still in Prague – asked me to stop off in the capital on my way back to Italy. I cautiously accepted. 'You'll see', he said, 'maybe it's more beautiful than before, because it's been restored. But it looks like Salzburg.' By this comparison he was telling me that Prague had lost its soul and its mystery: it was now like any handsome and good-humoured Austrian city; its demonic atmosphere, with its spectres of magi and alchemists from the age of King Rudolph, had vanished, leaving behind only bunches of mass-produced puppets on every street corner alongside the T-shirts; the arcana and cabals and golems were all gone, and the spirit of Rabbi Loew no longer roamed the narrow lanes of Josefov, the world's most famous ghetto, now filled with the exhaust fumes of American tourist coaches.

For me and nearly all my generation, Prague was not so much the haunt of Arcimboldo and Kafka, Hašek, Apollinaire and the Čapek brothers, or the golems of Lothar and Wegener, as the city of Stalin and Dubček, the main location of the organizations representing proletarian internationalism, the place where we encountered the hopes of the world and later the armoured cars of the Soviet army. The setting for all that was among the medieval towers of the Old Town, on the slopes of Malá Strana, beside the Vltava flowing in from the forests of Bohemia, where we went on boat trips, and on Vyšehrad, the rocky hill above the river, where it is said that the legendary Princess Libuše brought to an end the golden age of the rule of women, sages and magi.

The magic was dispelled by the time of my return in 1996, and I couldn't say whether this was due to the twenty years of Husák's rule or to the five of actually existing capitalism. The city was now given over to a swarm of tourists who transformed it into a street fair. The *vinarne*, the old wine bars, had turned into pizzerias, their Italian flags wedged between the medieval rosettes of the gateways on Neruda Street (named after Jan Neruda, the Czech poet who lived at No. 47 in the nineteenth century). But the new owners who occupied U zeleného krále, reluctant to wipe out the illustrious origins of their establishment, had a sign recalling its founding in 1608 placed alongside the Italian tricolour.

I couldn't even find the old cafés. The most famous, the Slavia, had been closed for some time, a victim of excessive faith in capital. The Academy of Fine Arts, whose building had played host to the café, leased it to a manager from Chicago, but he failed to pay the rent and it was sealed up on the orders of a court which, I was told, had been unable to reach a judgement for three years.

My memory lanes in the Old City – the little streets of Celetná, Pařížská or Maiselova – were all building sites, where houses and shops bought for a song in the early rush of the 1990s were being revamped and resold at astronomical prices. Rare old shops had given way to glittering Versace, Yves Saint-Laurent and Benetton boutiques, while those not yet renovated were host to bazaars selling Oriental clothes and jeans.

As tourism was the only economic interest here, the oldest parts were now the most modern. They had become the city centre again, supplanting Václavské náměstí, where Wenceslas, the patron saint of Bohemia, looked down from his imposing steed on a square that had become characterless since politics, for good or ill, deserted the country. It always used to be the focus of popular participation, drawing crowds of demonstrators from the founding of the Republic in 1918 through the post-Munich days in 1939, when Czechoslovakia was girding itself for a German invasion, or the exuberant welcoming of the Red Army as liberators in 1945, to the Youth Festival of 1947, the events of 1968 when Soviet troops stunned everyone by returning to crush the hopes of the Prague Spring, the annual floral commemorations, defying the threat of repression, at the spot where Jan Palach burned himself alive in 1969 like a Vietnamese bonze, and, most recently, the days of the Velvet Revolution in 1989.

The great rectangular space of the square was now degraded and marginalized, its pavements abandoned to crass visitors looking for the non-stop casinos that occupied nearly every second building. The largest of these was directly beneath the Hotel Yalta, once an emblem of the Communist regime. The presence of Coca-Cola was ubiquitous, reaching even into the lobby of the legendary Hotel Europa, where a huge automat dispensing American drinks – a red-and-white installation next to the porter's desk – blotted out the pastel shades of the splendid Jugendstil door leading to the secluded jewel of a dining room.

A little further on, in the gardens behind the railway station, I found the hallmarks of globalization: a great gathering of all kinds of poor, including Slavs from the far-flung East and thousands of Gypsies and Romanians hired by the charge hands of the modern construction industry. There they found refuge as temporary workers in the folds of a society which, though not affluent, had the lowest rate of unemployment in Europe – a society with relatively efficient structures and a skilled workforce, capable of offering excellent profits to German capital in search of low-wage conditions.

The city in which I arrived that August, in 1947, was very different indeed, but I was able to enjoy it less than those who had come only for the Festival. For Pucci Piccinato and I had the honour of being part of the delegation to the Council of the International Union of Students (IUS), and its meetings went on so long that we ended up missing the most exciting shows put on by the city. I was so proud of my first political role that I would not have skipped a session for anything in the world.

We were accommodated in Titova College – an austere student hostel from the old days that had been renamed after the Yugoslav leader. It was in the canteen there, on 9 August, that I celebrated my eighteenth birthday, in mixed company from which no continent was missing. (My diary recorded it with multiple exclamation marks: 'Now I am eighteen!!!!!')

Several days later, on 15 August, the Council suspended its morning session to hear an Indian delegate report that his country had been declared independent – the first colony to become an ex-colony. Those who had made it possible were two men called Gandhi and Nehru; it sounded to me as if they were related to Sandokan, since Salgari's India was the only one I knew.* A freckled, red-skinned youngster from the Communist Party of Great Britain spoiled the celebrations, however, by warning us that the whole thing was a sham cooked up by British imperialism.

Not everything went smoothly at the Council meetings, although I must confess that the meaning of many things escaped me. Pucci understood rather more than I – and explained it to me afterwards – because after a few days she had a fling with none other than the IUS general secretary, the Englishman Tom Madden. Officially he was a medical student, but in fact he had been travelling the world for two years in an attempt to unite all students in a single organization with the 'correct orientation'.

Although the incidents were connected with the rift opening up in the world, they were varied in nature – never explicitly political, always apparently more to do with procedural matters. For example, the exotically named Credentials Commission, a shadowy but powerful body, refused to recognize the legitimacy of the Italian delegation, on the grounds that there was no clearly defined national students' union in Italy that it could be said to represent. Four of the eight delegates (Pucci and I were only observers) walked out and slammed the door behind them, denouncing what they saw as a stitch-up by the Communists to exclude the non-Communists. To tell the truth, they all looked like Communists to me – but since the

---

* The pirate Sandokan, whose adventures took him to India among other countries, was the protagonist of eleven novels by the Italian writer Emilio Salgari (1862–1911).

four who said they weren't made an unfavourable impression on me, I didn't pay too much attention to the affair. Similar incidents involving the French and the British were reported to me by Pucci, who was now privy to secrets at the top. Indeed, the British disputed Tom's legitimacy as general secretary: he had been nominated to the post as a representative of the National Union of Students (a well-structured organization going back decades, with an orientation generally rather more moderate than his), but in the meantime the NUS had elected a new president, Bill Rust (the first non-Communist since 1930, I later learned), with the result that Tom's mandate had officially ceased to apply and, in the view of the NUS leadership, he was no longer entitled to hold the position he did at international level.

I found the exclusion of the Swiss more difficult to understand. I was told they had insisted on calling themselves 'neutral', in accordance with their country's traditions. But was it possible to be neutral in today's world? No, the Credentials Commission decreed; those who claimed to be neutral made themselves ineligible, since the IUS was lined up against Fascism and colonialism and in favour of peace. (Since then, I have to admit, whenever I hear the word 'neutral' – a concept that was not so bad in the later era of military blocs – I feel an immediate mistrust.)

Despite everything, the vote was unanimous in the end. This was partly due to the oratory of Joseph Grohman, the courteous fair-haired Czech president of the IUS – a man who was no longer exactly youthful, having spent five years in prison under the Germans.

He was not so old, however, as to avoid being caught up in the horrors of the Seventies. Marginalized in 1952 – maybe because the future dissident Artur London had been a witness at his wedding –

he was later rehabilitated and even appointed a vice-minister. But his life continued to follow the zigzags of his country's doleful Communist history: the Husák regime arrested him after '68 because of his close friendship with Aleksandr Shelepin, the Soviet vice-president at that IUS Council meeting in 1947, then head of the KGB, who, though a member of the CPSU secretariat under Khrushchev, gradually lost his power after the author of the Secret Speech was replaced by Brezhnev.

The Pucci-and-Tom story lasted longer than expected, so over the next few years she had ways of following the turbulence behind the scenes of the IUS and the devastating impact that the Czechoslovak coup d'état of February 1948 had upon the Prague-based organization.

Everything exploded at the 1950 Congress, when the Korean War was already underway, the Vietminh were making their mark on history, and Halstead Holman, the American vice-president of the IUS – who in reality represented scarcely any American students – was about to be hauled before the House Committee on Un-American Activities and charged inter alia with not having compared the USSR to Hitler's Germany.

In France, too, a new wind was blowing. Gérard de Bernis had been forced to give up his position as UNEF* secretary-general because, in circumstances unclear to me, he had openly applauded the North Korean delegation; and one of the IUS vice-presidents, Pierre Trouvat – a hefty individual with a keen wit, nicknamed 'Trouvat–Ho Chi Minh' by his detractors – was similarly squeezed out for having taken part in a demonstration at the Sorbonne that unfurled the Vietnamese flag. Tom himself,

---

* Union Nationale des Étudiants Français.

despite his authority and persuasiveness, was finally removed as a representative of British students, and stood accused of being a crypto-Communist.

In 1950 I arrived at the IUS Congress in Prague just in time to witness its implosion as an all-embracing international organization. I had made my way there from London, where I had gone for the summer with the first man with whom I had an adult relationship, an American painter who benefited from one of the fantastic study grants available to war veterans. I almost fled from him – I couldn't bear that he knew nothing about Europe – but I decided to sacrifice my cumbersome virginity to him precisely because he lived so far away and I didn't risk having to take on any commitment. Finally, I left London on my own, hitchhiking all the way to Prague on a long route via France, Switzerland and Austria (it was still impossible to cross occupied Germany without special permission).

After the 1950 Congress, the IUS was left representing students in the Socialist bloc and a few parts of the Third World, as well as Western Communists and Italian Socialists. Official organizations in the West that had not already done so broke with the IUS, accepting the invitation from Olof Palme – present as an observer from the Swedish Union of Students – to gather in Stockholm to found an alternative international body with a permanent secretariat: the International Students Conference (COSEC), which never acquired major importance.

We did not mince our words, and branded the splitters as CIA agents – a natural enough charge if one thinks that, apart from 'us' and 'them', Third World liberation movements were also appearing on the scene. This was the point on which we drew the battle lines: one was either with them – and therefore, in those days, with the USSR – or one was against them. Nor is it an accident that the COSEC blew apart in the 1960s, when students in the United States were beginning to speak of American imperialism in connection with the Vietnam War.

Despite the stormy atmosphere, the 1950 Congress observed all the liturgical niceties, including the offering of gifts to foreign students by workers' organizations in the host country. The North Koreans got an ambulance, the Chinese a bicycle, and we Italians a bust of Stalin.

I was unable to attend subsequent congresses and do not know what happened at them. For a few years, beginning in 1952, the police headquarters in Rome denied me a passport because of my first two court sentences following arrests of the kind that were a frequent occurrence during those years.

In 2007 Giovanni Berlinguer – who succeeded Tom Madden as general secretary of the IUS – rang me up and said: 'Guess who's here with me? Tom Madden.' I hadn't set eyes on him since that congress more than half a century earlier, and I didn't know what had become of him after his romance with Pucci burned itself out. The former 'mole' had finally become a doctor in the United States and married an American woman. He was passing through Rome, and by a stroke of good fortune had found Giovanni's address.

When he continued on his way, he left us a book that caused us much laughter: *Students and the Cold War*, published in the United States in 1996 by Joel Kotek, a rather anti-Communist historian teaching at the Université Libre in Brussels. It related in great detail, with documents to hand, the story of the international student organizations during the key period from 1945 to 1952 – from the end of anti-Fascist unity to the Cold War. In particular, it showed that all the student leaders involved in the historic Western split of 1950 had been in the pay of the CIA (either personally or via their organizations), and later also of MI5 and the Deuxième Bureau; and that, right from the beginning, the embassies of the respective countries, in close touch with one another, had established a network of spies to keep tabs on each and every student who crossed the Iron Curtain physically and politically – that is, to check on what they said, did and wrote.

We laughed because for some time all three of us had mocked our previous subordination to the propaganda of 'actually existing socialism' and repented of our defining the splitters as 'CIA agents'. Yet now it turned out that the propaganda had been true!

The author considered this normal, arguing that many Communists had taken orders from secret services in the East. In the West, though, it had been a question of political parties – which was something different. There was a very cold, sometimes almost hot, war under way, and no one was inclined to be over-particular in supporting their chosen ideology. How else is it thinkable that a man like Olof Palme – the courageous head of government who defied the American arms drive of the 1970s and 1980s, the prime minister alongside whom I often fought on peace issues during those years – could once have been a CIA agent?

DIRTY GLASSES

Giovanni Berlinguer, the head of the Italian delegation to that first IUS Council in 1947, was so serious that I felt truly in awe of him. He had a tooth abscess that hurt like hell, and so he asked me to go with him and speak with the dentist in German (the foreign language most widely used in Czechoslovakia at the time). But, to the dentist's consternation, he insisted that the offending tooth should be extracted forthwith, even though it could easily have been saved:

he could not afford to remain in pain for any more days, since his duties required him to be in full command of his faculties.

Giovanni's sacrifice of his tooth for the sake of politics made a deep impression on me, but it was only the first lesson in austerity during the crash course in Communist literacy that I underwent in that summer of 1947.

After the end of the IUS Council, I heard it said that an international brigade of volunteers was being formed in Prague to help in the construction of a railway in Yugoslavia. It was an opportunity for me to acquaint myself better with the still turbulent events in Trieste, and so I decided at once to put my name forward.

No one knew for sure when the brigade would leave, but it seemed to be some days away. I had to find the means of surviving until then, once my comrades in the delegation were on their way back to Rome and the festival was closing down. So I accepted the proposal of three British delegates – Duncan Wood, Tony Simmons and Walter Davis – to join them on a trip round the country: an 'autostop' trip, as they put it. I pretended to understand what they meant, although in reality it was the first time I had heard the word.

It proved to be an invaluable lesson for me, since over the coming years I would use this means of travel widely and frequently all over Europe, as naturally as if I was taking the train. But it was not the best option in Czechoslovakia in 1947. The war was not long over, private cars could be counted on the fingers of one hand, and the roads were narrow and in bad repair. We had to wait for long periods at a time on the Bohemian high plain between Prague and Plzen (its name known to us from Pilsen lager), a stretch that passed through the legendary spa resorts of Karlovy Vary and Mariánské Lázně, which my aunts had visited in the days when they were known as Karlsbad and Marienbad. The only vehicles that seemed to come and go were ramshackle trucks loaded with hay. But on the other hand, local farmers made us feel welcome and allowed us to spend the night in their haylofts. At mealtimes, Duncan pulled from his pockets a chunk of bread, a little jar of jam and a jack-knife so dirty that it made me waver between hunger and hygienic abstinence.

When we returned to Prague after four days on the road, a special court consisting of the top people in the Italian delegation was waiting to sit in judgement on my unseemly behaviour: I, a lone woman, had run off with three Englishmen.

Giuliano Pajetta, the most senior of the PCI figures still there, was assigned to give me a dressing-down. Summoned to appear before him, I listened to his speech but understood almost nothing from his references to a discussion between Lenin and Clara Zetkin about dirty glass rims to which no one would want to press his lips. I didn't know who she was, nor had I much idea of who he was either, and in any case I couldn't grasp the meaning of those glasses – partly because I was so innocent (the only girl who didn't lose her virginity in Prague that summer) that I needed Luciana Franzinetti, the future wife of Ugo Pecchioli, to explain to me that it was a question of multiple sexual relations.

Despite this clarification from Luciana – who became my super-ego when I later joined the PCI – I still failed to understand how a hitchhiking trip could make people think I would go to bed with just anyone. From Trieste I had got a Central European education, open to camaraderie between males and females but also very puritanical. The PCI, however, was imbued with popular Catholic culture – that was another discovery for me.

I tried, without success, to explain myself to Giuliano Pajetta. In the end he may have taken pity on my perplexity, for, without continuing to recommend Clara Zetkin, he offered me Ilf and Petrov's *Il paese di Dio* by way of consolation.*

Over the next few days I was subjected to even more tiresome trials. I no longer had a roof over my head at Titova College, because the delegates to the IUS Council were immediately replaced there by members of the Council of the World Federation of Democratic Youth (WFDY). This was the international organization that also included workers and farmers (still the overwhelming majority in the Italian Communist Youth): one need only think of the Chinese to appreciate that it had hundreds of millions of members.

The head of the Italian delegation to the WFDY was the other Berlinguer brother, Enrico, already an important PCI leader and even more austere than Giovanni. He had to share his room with a childhood friend of mine, Bubi Campos (later one of the most important Italian city planners), who was not yet a PCI member but was one of the few outside the Communist and Socialist parties to have accepted a position of responsibility in the international organizations supported by Moscow.

Being of no fixed abode, I asked Bubi to clear the wash basin in their room a little; he then obliged me by fixing a wire from wall to wall and allowing me to hang some hurriedly washed bras and knickers there. These evidently made Enrico Berlinguer suspect intimate relations between me and the other occupant of the room; once more I was grappling with the glasses of Lenin and Clara Zetkin.

Nor was that all. Not knowing where to sleep that night, I went

---

* For an English translation of the original Russian *Odnoetazhnaia Amerika*, see Ilya Ilf and Evgeny Petrov, *Ilf and Petrov's American Road Trip*, ed. Erika Wolf (New York: Princeton Architectural Press, 2007).

knocking on the door of the college where a student delegation from Rome's faculty of medicine was being put up by their counterparts in Prague. I knew one of the delegates, Laura Frontali: she was the daughter of the paediatrician who had looked after me from birth, the upright and celebrated Professor Gino Frontali, whose membership of the Communist Party became known to me only after the war. I was sure that Laura would help me find a place to stay – and indeed she did. But since there was no spare room in the women's quarters, she put me on a folding bed in the men's section, where her fiancé among others had been allocated.

I was very tired and couldn't stay awake until the others returned, so I found myself being dislodged in the middle of the night when they discovered to their horror that a girl had presumed to share their room. It was an inadmissible liberty.

I felt increasingly disturbed: I hadn't bargained on Communists being so narrow-minded. Once I joined the PCI, I had to face the fact that Maria Goretti, a girl of eleven murdered in 1902 by her would-be rapist, was one of the heroines of its youth movement.

AUGUST 1947: A TRIP THROUGH DEVASTATED EUROPE

Finally we set off for Yugoslavia, and I could say goodbye to my shaky life in Prague with no official address.

After all the postponements, we didn't trust the schedule we were given. But the practical instructions told us that this time it was for real, that there should no longer be any obstacles.

When I think back sixty years later, the delayed departure of the train seems laughably trivial: it cannot have been easy to get a convoy underway across the ravaged continent, carrying a few hundred specimens of the generation born between the wars in various parts of the globe. It was difficult to attribute a nationality to many of my companions, since their documents reflected a world soon to be swept away – the old colonial empires – and contained details which, though bureaucratically correct, no longer corresponded to the identity that their bearers proudly proclaimed and had often won for themselves, arms in hand.

My compartment was a microcosm of this epochal transition. There was a lively Indonesian who at the festival had represented the guerrilla movement that drove the Dutch colonialists out of his country. A few weeks earlier, however, on 26 July, the liberation fighters had had to take up arms again, since the former rulers had left behind some troops to watch over the newly won rights. He exchanged hugs with Jan van Minnen, a painter from Amsterdam, who supported the Indonesians in their struggle. There was a Vietnamese, from a country which, to tell the truth, I scarcely knew existed, representing a similar guerrilla movement against domination by the democratic French Republic. And there was an Indian with his female companion. They were the most legitimate of all, since their country had obtained independence just two weeks earlier; but bureaucracy moves more slowly than politics, and their documents had not yet caught up with events: they were still subjects of His Britannic Majesty.

There were no Chinese on our train, but everyone was talking about their epic struggle – even if we knew little or nothing of the details. As for Africa, it did not exist, being divided between the ultra-French 'Territoires d'outre-mer' and the British and Portuguese colonies. Latin America was almost absent, such a long way from our blood-stained continent, but also from the euphoria of the brave new world we imagined to be within reach.

There were large numbers of Europeans, all with their documents in order but – on account of their beards, clothes and manners – looking as if they had just stepped out of a cave.

We spent many hours with our rucksacks on the station platform in Prague, eyeing one another up inquisitively. The only faces I recognized, almost familiar to me by now, were those of Tony Simmons and Duncan Wood, two of the three Englishmen with whom I had tried out hitchhiking in Czechoslovakia, much to the irritation of the PCI. They would be on the same express going east, although they would not stay on it all the way to Yugoslavia.

When the train finally arrived, we managed to find places in the same compartment amid the crowd. I knew I could rely on plain bread and jam, and from time to time they would produce some along with their one filthy knife. Had it not been for them, I'd have gone hungry for the three days that the train took to pass through areas of Europe left ruined when the war had ended two years before. The signs were still visible, as if it had been yesterday: piles of rubble everywhere, along the improbable railway line that carried us from Prague to Belgrade via Bratislava and Budapest.

We proceeded in stages. Made necessary by the state of the track, the slowness was actually welcome because it allowed us enough time to take a look at the cities en route. From Bratislava – today no longer part of Czechoslovakia but the capital of a different country – I even managed to send a picture postcard that now lies in one of my mother's boxes. Dated 23 August 1947, the old photo shows the bulk of a Hotel Carlton that no longer exists; the stamp, bearing the image of Jan Masaryk, cost 1.20. I ask myself which currency this was, and which currency we used in the various countries. There must have existed a kind of de facto 'euro'.

I wrote that I was about to enter Hungary and that it was extraordinary to be travelling with a brigade consisting of citizens of fifteen different countries. I greeted my family with a 'collective hug', but immediately added – to be on the safe side and not to frighten them unduly – that the word 'collective' was not meant in any political sense ('I don't write it because I've picked up some idea of the masses here').

Another Englishman was travelling with us – and benefiting from the largesse of Tony and Duncan. In fact, he was no longer British but Canadian, and his family origins were Hungarian; he was going to Budapest to look for some relatives. He was studying physics at Toronto University, and only many years later did I discover that the name he wrote in my address book – Polanyi – was actually very well known. John was the nephew of the great Karl Polanyi, the author of *The Great Transformation*, which helped me so much to understand the nature of the capitalism that we were experiencing.

(When I first set foot in Toronto five decades later, I knew that John was teaching at the university and tried to track him down, just as I have so many others who appeared and disappeared from my life all those years ago and who must have kept a record of my name somewhere or other. Encounters from that period have remained an indelible memory: they were part of my discovery of the world, after the long ghettoization of Fascism and the war, suddenly bursting forth in an astonishing variety of colours. When I found John, his voice thinner from age, he recognized me at once. And at once we began recalling together that wonderful train journey from Prague to Belgrade.)

We were crossing Central Europe – the legendary *Mitteleuropa*, as people at home had always called the places which now seemed so unlike the image of them passed on to me. It was 1947: the Iron Curtain was not yet in place, but the 'iciness' between West and East was already palpable. None of us really knew what it was all about – I, a complete novice, less than any of the others. We liked all the red flags we saw along the way; they told us that socialism was conquering the world, and we felt good about that.

At night we slept in the luggage nets or on the floor, huddled together against the cold. At dawn on the second day, the train slowly came to a halt on a dead-end track in an almost deserted station. It was Budapest.

They told us we could leave our things on the train: we had a day to see the city, before the train left again at eight in the evening. See you then, the railwaymen said.

I was thrilled to bits. Here was Budapest: the city of so many Medusa mystery novels (the green-cover series already going in the days of Fascism); the city of the 1848 uprisings against the Habsburg Empire (as in Trieste), of operetta and of family trips from nearby Venezia Giulia. It reminded me of Nino's and Mother's last holiday – in 1935, I think – in the famous six-cylinder Bianchi that would be demoted to a van during the war. I saw in my mind's eye the labels stuck on their luggage at various hotels, the photos, and even a few films (still among my treasures today) shot by Nino's dilettante hand with one of the new mini cine cameras. What they captured, in photos or on now worn celluloid, no longer exists: wartime bombs blew it away, together with the historical period of which it was part.

I could not find that Budapest when I stopped in the city with my new friends: a few vestiges of Buda, on its hill, but almost nothing of old Pest. We spent a whole day wandering around, or sitting enchanted on the banks of the Danube and eating bread and jam from British pockets. There was no other food in sight – even if we had had the money to buy it.

The next dawn found us in another railway siding, this time in the deserted, semi-ruined station in Belgrade. Another 'tourist stop' amid ruins and hunger – then off again. At night, with the aid of the moon, we glimpsed high arid mountains and valleys no larger than gullies, along which the track wound its way between Serbia and Bosnia. These were sacred sites of the Titoist resistance: the British knew most about this and told us of its heroic feats. Then, finally, we pulled into our destination: Sarajevo.

It was the first really exotic city I had seen in my life. I wrote more about it in letters home than in my diary, describing, sometimes also drawing, veiled women with Turkish-style trousers, small, colourful alleyways, and the cafés on every corner where waiters poured a fearsome brew from tiny coffee pots into even tinier cups.

YUGOSLAVIA: THE CAMP AT ZENICA

That summer we never had a chance to return to Sarajevo, because a train took us on the narrow-gauge track to Zenica, and from there ten kilometres north to the site where we were to help build a modern railway line between Šamac and Sarajevo, in place of the old one left by the Austro-Hungarian Empire. Pictures of Broz Tito were everywhere. He was the first Communist leader who really bowled me over: I knew rather little about Palmiro Togliatti, partly because his life seemed less daring and more like that of a professor, whereas Tito was strikingly handsome, with his military beret and its red star.

The work camp consisted of three or four wooden barracks: one housed international and the others Yugoslav participants (a total of six thousand young people); students from Zagreb were in the one closest to us. For sleeping, there was just the tiled floor – not even a straw mattress – with a blanket to protect us from the biting cold of the Bosnian mountains. The few women – one each from Canada and Britain plus myself – slept in a separate room, together with an Indian couple who didn't want to be apart.

As in Prague, an episode of sexual segregation revealed a side of my country that I had not previously suspected. It happened after I had been there a couple of weeks, when we were told that one of the Italian brigades further north would be passing through our camp on its way home and would need somewhere to sleep for a few nights until onward transport was available.

Our leader, an English bricklayer called Bill Horn, decided that we should send a delegation to welcome them at the junction a few kilometres away. He asked me to act as interpreter – a role I found rather difficult, since I had arrived in Yugoslavia without any English, and my two foreign languages, German and French, were of little or no use. Still, I'd managed out of sheer necessity to acquire a smattering of English, since it was the only common medium and there were no other Italians with me.

The Italian brigade arrived in disarray: its leader, a former partisan from Bologna, was almost at the rear rather than the front of the column, hobbling along the path; they were all loaded with bags, looking more like refugees than activists. Their tattered flag put the dampeners on our official welcome, and I generally felt a little let down.

But the worst was yet to come. Bill had decided that the Italians should spend their two nights with us in the room housing our latest arrivals: a group of British girls. However, the brigade commander from Bologna would not hear of this: it's impossible, he said, because we are all male. Dismay and astonishment among the international students, obstinate refusal among the Italians.

In the end, after hours of work that seemed like time-wasting amid the demands of postwar reconstruction, a temporary partition was put up to separate the sexes for the next forty-eight hours. Nevertheless, under the cover of night, more than one Italo-British couple dispensed with a screen among the bushes along the river bank.

The arrival of the Italians did bring some festive elements, especially into the cuisine. For four weeks we had been eating nothing but beans – I hated them and the act of swallowing them was my first sacrifice for the sake of Communism – and powdered egg, shipped in large tins by the United Nations Relief Agency to the starving young Yugoslav Republic. The Italians, on the other hand – I don't know how or why – had been provided with large supplies of spaghetti, and in the evening they offered everyone a pasta banquet.

The comrade in charge of the kitchen was a real cook, having learned the art at his father's trattoria in Prati, in Rome. For us to be on friendly terms, though, I had to get over a highly embarrassing incident for him and his friend, the sub-cook. Thinking at first that I wasn't Italian, the chef took one look at me and said aloud with an assumption of impunity: 'Not bad at all, that English girl.' 'Come off it', the other replied, 'can't you see how skinny she is!'

The sub-chef was Luigi Ficcadenti. A few months later, on 12 October 1947, the very day when I decided to join the PCI, he and other Communist Youth members in the Esquilino district were arrested and charged with involvement in the stabbing of Gervasio Federici, a Christian Democrat who had been sticking up posters near Piazza Vittorio for the first local elections in Rome. Federici – according to the right-wing papers – had refused to shout 'Viva il comunismo!', as the Communist rabble had ordered him to do.

Luigi served three years in prison, together with his fourteen-year-old brother Marcello and a young worker called Alfredo Pozzi; the nature of the provocation in which they had been caught up would never be known. Nor did Luigi ever fully recover from his teenage imprisonment. On his release, he worked as a proofreader at *L'Unità* and then at *Nuova Generazione*, the FGCI weekly that I edited between the late Fifties and the early Sixties.

Camp life was hard at Zenica. Waking up at five, we had half an hour of gymnastics, led by a young Dutch pastor who had somehow or other ended up in our brigade; then ablutions in the icy water of a stream that flowed into the Bosna river; then breakfast (starvation rations) and a three-kilometre march through forest to the post assigned to us on the new stretch of railway. There we had to build the embankment on which the sleepers would later be placed, first digging the stony material from among the bramble, loading it onto old carts that weighed hundreds of kilos empty, and clambering with them to the roadbed. (Italo Calvino wrote in one of his letters to *L'Unità* about the voluntary work brigades: 'If anyone thinks it was just token work, they are greatly mistaken …')

We had to trek up and down for five hours, beneath a sun that already scorched you in the morning, with only a short break to drink something. There was even a kind of time-keeper, to monitor our individual productivity. I got stuck into it and within a month, despite a number of blisters, managed to become an *udarnička* [shock worker]: the Serbo-Croat equivalent of 'Stakhanovite'. I was even awarded a special red badge at a highly serious closing ceremony, where we were told that our labours had allowed the goal to be achieved. The new 240-kilometre railway, with its seventeen bridges and two-and-a-half kilometres of tunnels, was on the point of completion.

I was bursting with pride.

*　　　*　　　*

Having jealously guarded the *udarnička* badge, I eventually lost it. I do still have the paper diploma, though: a veritable baptism certificate that ushered me into a new life. The experience also made me understand how the effort of manual labour eats up your energy, and I think back to it today whenever there is a discussion of pensions and exhausting work.

Out of curiosity, I recently googled the words *Omladinska pruga*, thinking that I would find nothing. But three entries came up:

(1) *Omladinska pruga*, 'Youth Railway', is the name of a DVD marketing company based in Belgrade.

(2) To celebrate its sixtieth anniversary, a trip for veterans of the Šamac-Sarajevo line was organized in October 2007. The ex-volunteers – some thirty or so – took part in the event, at the invitation of an 'Italian coordination group for Yugoslavia', which I had never heard of before. The website contained comments by various participants. A certain Fadil, who attended the ceremony with his grandson, writes: 'In those days we were prepared for the hardest work, with a song on our lips, whereas now people aren't even up to clearing the snow in front of their block of flats.' And Ivan adds: 'They were great times; people would sing songs, happy and proud. Glad to have helped rebuild Yugoslavia, on the rubble of the war of liberation. Nowadays, any young punk thinks he has a right to laugh at our effort, at our contribution to the achievement of fraternity.'

(3) Under the heading *Omladinska pruga*, a kind of online Croat eBay – www.aukcije.hr – announced that a certificate of participation (*legitimacija*) in the Youth Railway would be auctioned between 31 July and 7 August 2008. Base price: $42.50, sold by 'Phoenix'. I did not enter the bidding, because I still have one of those documents, but I confess that I would have parted with a small fortune if a real *udarnička* badge had been on offer.

AROUND THE CAMPFIRE

Evenings in Zenica were wonderful. There I acquired nearly the whole of my basic store of knowledge – a mountain of information that filled the void in which I had lived during the war. The world suddenly appeared vast, my Via Vallisneri, in Parioli, positively minute.

We would gather around a fire, where everyone would talk about their own country. For me, who scarcely knew what France was, the stories were a tremendous education. Little by little, I wrote hurried letters home about them – letters on notepaper headed 'Omladinska pruga, Šamac-Sarajevo' – hoping to infect them with my enthusiasm and to obtain forgiveness for presenting my Yugoslav adventure as a fait accompli, after my travelling companions in Prague had returned to Rome and told them I had gone off to build a railway in the Balkans.

From Prague onward, I no longer had much desire – nor, above all, much time – to write my diary. There were too many new things and emotions to record; I felt as if a wave had swept me away, filling me with a desperate need to keep my head above water. Since then, in any case, the keeping of a diary has seemed to me a childish activity.

In that summer of 1947, the world was taking on a new look. But the great postwar transformation had not yet occurred, and traces of a past that would soon disappear altogether were still present. In the brigade album that we took home as a souvenir of our endeavours, everyone signed alongside their name and country of origin – sometimes mentioned with pride, even if it had not yet been born or was destined to vanish in less than a year. Palestine, for instance, was written next to the signature of a Jewish girl, Lena Schwartz. It was a land about which I had previously had only a little information, after a day in 1946 when I had seen homemade posters on the walls along Via Nazionale and asked what they were about. They had borne the imprint of Irgun Zvai Leumi and protested against the refusal of British imperialism to allow Jews to emigrate to Palestine. This was enough for me to feel immediate solidarity with Lena when I got to know her in the Yugoslav brigade

I have never met Lena Schwartz since that time, but I have often wondered how she experienced the mutation of Palestine into the State of Israel in 1948. On the other hand, I have seen again Myrtle Canin, a white South African. The face of the speaker seemed familiar to me at an anti-apartheid demonstration in London in the Eighties, and at the end we recognized each other. We hadn't set eyes on each other for forty years, and the roads that we had taken since Zenica took a long time to relate.

Zenica, even more than Prague, made me feel a stupid little bourgeois girl, provincial and ignorant. For that reason too, I worked hard to become an *udarnička*: it was a way of winning pardon for what I was.

Some evenings they showed us films in the camp – early works of the new Yugoslav cinema. All of them were about the Resistance. Unfailingly there was a scene in which someone shouted: 'Italianski!' – and then machine-guns would open up on my ambushed fel-low-countrymen. I tried to melt into the darkness, feeling all the more ashamed because in Zenica I had discovered another dark side to my country. For in the late seventeenth century, our hero Prince Eugene of Savoy mounted a series of barbaric attacks that destroyed Zenica and a few other towns in the area, where it seems that Serbs, Muslims, Croats and Jews had been living peacefully together.

It is extraordinary how much correspondence I have found in boxes at home from those months in 1947 – a pile of letters to Italy from the various obscure addresses of my work camps and colleges, as well as some that reached me from Rome despite my moving around in war-devastated Europe. I came across a very sharp one in which Father wrote: 'You are crazy. That wouldn't matter if you didn't cause so much concern to those who love you. We are very worried and beg you to come back home at once, also because all the Italians have now returned from Prague and you are alone, who knows where.'

In fact, I decided in Bosnia to enrol for a second period of work, so that my brigade comrades showed up before me at Via Vallisneri on their way home via Italy. Mother describes their visit in one of her letters – half angry, half curious about my new world – which also reached me in the camp. She says that three of my friends, one Belgian, one Australian and one *pankistan* [sic], called round. 'They showed me photos of the camp and we became outright friends. The *pankistan* made me laugh a lot and asked questions of colossal naivety; the Australian rarely spoke, while the Belgian chattered non-stop and was so effusive that, on his way out, he said we were the nicest family he had ever known. Grandmother, who sobbed when she saw you in the photos, gave each of them a rose from the garden. A young lady from South Africa also phoned, but she didn't actually come. Now comes the best part. I was putting some potatoes in a box when I saw a strange man at the gate. I told the maid to give him a piece of bread. Fortunately he got a word in first and asked: Luciana Castellina here? My mind opened, and with it the gate. Kuty [our dog] barked like a maniac; I smiled as I asked myself what kind of language I should use to speak with this man. Do you know who he was? The commander of your brigade, an English bricklayer, told me interesting things about you, but our conversation was laboured because of language. I offered him a glass of cognac. He was dead tired; he had in his hand a map of Rome and St Peter's and had been running around like mad looking for Via Vallisneri.'

I still feel ashamed that it didn't occur to Mother or anyone else to give my brigade comrades what they all desperately needed: something to eat! Something other than roses and cognac!

A little more fortunate was the last arrival, Willie Nordrå, a Norwegian who later became famous in his country as a painter. Mother wrote to me that she offered him some pasta and that, dispensing with cutlery, he bit into it directly on the plate. He had never seen spaghetti before.

Since those days I have returned three times to Zenica. The first, in the late 1970s, was as a member of a delegation from my party, the PdUP-Manifesto, which had been invited to Yugoslavia by the League of Communists. What had been little more than a village was by then a large industrial centre, with chimney stacks all around. By the river, formerly open country, a little museum displayed many photos of our epic railway feat.

The second occasion was in the late 1990s, immediately after the war that laid waste to Bosnia. Zenica had been one of its epicentres and my heart had missed a beat each of the dozens of times I heard it mentioned; Tuzla, better known, was a short distance away. There was so much rubble. Only the mosque was intact. It was the first time I had seen one in my life, back in 1947, when we went to visit the town on an afternoon off; I remember that the little train slowed down, but did not come to a halt, when we got off and later got back on again. I had been hugely curious about that kind of strange church where you had to remove your shoes before entering it.

Dany Cohn-Bendit and I were accompanying Yehudi Menuhin to Sarajevo, where he was to give a concert for the opening of the newly rebuilt National Theatre. I took the opportunity to make a brief side-trip to Zenica, but there was no longer any trace of the voluntary brigades museum in the war-torn landscape. Our railway was dead – to be reactivated only in 2003 – and no one knew our anthem: 'Jedan dva, jedan dva, Omladinska pruga, omladinska titova…' ('One two, one two, Youth Railway, Tito's Youth…').

The third time I revisited Zenica, in the summer of 2009, was on the occasion of the Sarajevo Film Festival, where Serb, Croat, Bosniak and Slovene filmmakers worked happily with one another despite all that had happened. The small town that once hosted my old work camp – like the capital of the new republic of Bosnia and Herzegovina – was now blooming and unrecognizable. But it was impossible to find any traces there of our past. In Sarajevo, the old General Jovan Divjak – commander-in-chief of Bosniak-Muslim forces during the war – took me to see the tunnels through which supplies had passed to the besieged city. And when I told him I had worked in the brigades, he embraced me and wept tears of emotion, recalling Tito with devastating nostalgia.

Our work then had been devoted to the new Yugoslavia, but the country had been all of a piece with Tito. Today, old people like my General Divjak are alone in remembering the legendary leader: the only one who freed his land from Nazi-Fascist occupation before the arrival of Allied troops; the national hero who bound the peoples of the northern Balkans closely together into a single internationally respected state; the Communist who refused to submit to Moscow, giving birth, with Nehru and Sukarno, to the Non-Aligned Movement, that extraordinary strategic invention which for decades loosened the grip of the two superpowers on the Third World.

WHOSE IS TRIESTE?

That autumn we discussed Trieste a great deal in the camp. The peace treaty with Italy had been signed a few months earlier: the contested area had become the Free Territory of Trieste, divided between Zone A, under Western control, and Zone B, under Yugoslav control. Everything was still undecided. Tito claimed Yugoslav sovereignty in the name of the majority-Slovene rural population, arguing that they held the advantage because what counted was the surrounding element, not the surrounded. For my part, I felt increasingly puzzled when the Tour of Italy was forbidden to include a Trieste section, on the grounds that it was the Tour of Italy and the city was no longer Italy.

Despite my unease, I felt good about the discussions. I had come to build the railway mainly in order to understand the Trieste question, which was then at the forefront of the international political confrontation and was especially important to me because of my Obidan grandfather. The crisis there was also the main factor that had led me to seek out the Communists.

In debates or private conversations, I was put severely to the test regarding the basic argument. 'It should be Yugoslav', they all said – especially the British, with a certain arrogance. 'You were all Fascists, whereas they lost a million and seven hundred thousand people in the war.' I was shaken: the Trieste I knew, and my family, were Italian. I still knew little about how the Fascists had treated the Slovenes, and only now was I beginning to understand the war that had led my country to occupy Yugoslavia and even to proclaim a member of the House of Savoy – them again – as viceroy. For me that war had meant only the death of my friend Marcello Cajoli in the mountains.

I didn't dare to contradict, but I was ill at ease and upset.

OCTOBER 1947: RETURN VIA TRIESTE

I was even more ill at ease when, after a short holiday in Dubrovnik as a reward for our contribution to the rebuilding of Yugoslavia, I finally arrived in Trieste. I was wearing, like everyone else, the brigade's brown cloth overalls – my only clothes after months of wandering – and I had my red *udarnička* badge pinned to the collar. I was sure that the railwaymen and porters at our arrival station would give us an enthusiastic welcome.

Their coldness was a slap in the face. I couldn't understand it. What I didn't know was that things had already grown considerably more complicated in Trieste.

In September, frontier posts had been moved to a new line running through villages, gardens and even cemeteries. There were also a number of serious incidents between demonstrators from opposing factions, as well as continual strikes. When a little girl was mown down by a machine-gun during a popular festival on the outskirts, official sources said the perpetrators were unknown, but each side put the blame on the others.

In Trieste, however, 'the others' now referred to complex forces: it was not just a question of Fascists and the Left; Communists too were split, not only between Yugoslavs and Italians but also among Italians themselves. Which counted for more: class, in whose name it was natural for a worker to side with a socialist society such as the Federal Republic of Yugoslavia; or nation, for which an Italian was supposed to want to remain in his own country? Only after I returned to Italy did I read Togliatti's wise words: 'Democracy is not like eating an artichoke: you can't peel off one leaf after another and then put them together in a more democratic community.' The question of class or nation left me incapable of coming up with an answer.

Once in Trieste, I didn't even have the money for a train to Rome. I was therefore forced to go to Aunt Ester's, in the old hillside villa overlooking the port, although I would have preferred not to so as to avoid the unpleasantness of political disagreements.

She sent the old chauffeur Oscar to pick me up at the station – the same man who had driven us through Italy to Venice on the day after the Liberation. He took me away from my group, which was still saying its farewells before dispersing to various destinations. He looked as if he had extracted me from a nest of cockroaches.

Before Aunt Ester said as much as hello to me, she sent me off 'to remove that stuff [the overalls] from your back' and to have a shower.

Despite the coldness of the Trieste railwaymen, Yugoslavia had been an exalting experience and shown me the huge energy involved in building a new and different country. I didn't exactly know how, but the Communism I had glimpsed for the first time close up had won me over.

A little more than six months later, at the Cinema Ausonia, I attended an activists' meeting of the Rome region of the PCI that I had joined in the meantime. There, with the gravity attending dramatic historical choices, Togliatti told us that Tito was a traitor.

4. DISCOVERING ITALY

THE DECISION

After my return from Yugoslavia, everything happened in a rush. I was bursting with emotions and new discoveries I wanted to share. But I suddenly felt that my nearest and dearest – family members, longstanding friends – were no longer true conversation partners. They listened, of course, but without understanding me, and in the end what I had to say did not really interest them. I realized, with indignation, that they did not even know India had become independent – a development I had learned of in Prague, which I now reported with a detached sense of superiority and with deep pity for those unaware of it.

Young people of my age seemed distracted by other things – university life, love affairs, and so on. Their world was no longer mine. In my journey across the most devastated part of Europe, I had discovered histories that never featured in the tiny slices taught at school, as well as a whole different scale of values and principles. And this shattered the universe in which I had lived until the age of eighteen. Towards those who had remained within it, I now felt an overwhelming estrangement that I could sense would be definitive. (And so it was – except in the case of more than a few friends who completed the same trajectory over subsequent years, even if at the time they were still suspicious of my mutation.)

New comrades – I learned to use this word and understood that it meant something more than friends – were not yet forthcoming in that autumn of 1947. I no longer had my school, Il Tasso, which had been the central reference point of my life in the last few years. University had not yet begun. So it was not easy for me to pick up the thread. I felt alone and ever more inadequate or superfluous; my arrogant self-assurance had vanished. I had learned to operate with a collective and to measure myself against it, so that now I felt abandoned after the months of intense communal life. It was no longer possible for me to sit and watch the world without doing anything. Indeed, it seemed immoral.

I looked for the people I had known in the Youth Front: the ones I had been with in Prague. But now they were all involved in the party – the PCI, of course, as the others had faded from the daily lives of my generation – and were up to their necks in the election campaign for the Rome municipality. If I opted for the PCI rather the PSI, it was mainly because I hardly knew anyone in the Socialists, still less in the Partito d'Azione. They were simply not a presence, and the few I did know seemed lesser than the Communists in every sense: less cultivated, less resolute, less active. Besides, the best of them were champing at the bit to join the PCI, held back by its leaders' tactical wish that they remain and keep the Socialist Left alive.

I timidly made contact with some Communists and asked if I could join too; I felt I would be forever useless outside the PCI. But I still had some reservations: one didn't join the Party light-heartedly; it meant a lifetime commitment, and for a long time it felt like a leap into the void.

I eventually overcame my hesitation largely out of rage at the events of 11 October 1947 on Piazza Vittorio, when Gervasio Federici was killed after two days of tension and clashes, and after a meeting that 'a certain Almirante'* – as I noted in my last diary entry – 'presumed to hold in the name of a reconstituted Fascist party'. Some young Communists – including Luigi Ficcadenti – were accused of the murder, but I was convinced of their innocence and felt sure that the whole thing was a murky plot on the part of the PCI's enemies.

On Via Ariosto a memorial slab still reads: 'On the eve of the vote which for the first time would result in a democratic Christian administration on Capitoline Hill, the young Gervasio Federici was stabbed because, aware of the danger and proud of the test, he affirmed his religious and political beliefs in the name of Immortal Rome.'

On the next day – when Romans went to the polls, though the age limit of twenty-one meant that I could not yet vote – I approached two Party members who seemed capable of dealing with my case: Alberto Caracciolo, secretary of the University Branch (later an illustrious historian and father of Lucio, the editor of the international affairs journal *Limes*); and Luciano Ventura, a rather severe student at the law faculty, where I had meanwhile enrolled. (I didn't choose philosophy, as I would have wished, because I was sure I would not be able to keep up, and because I wanted a degree that would allow me to earn my own living as quickly as possible and be completely free to make my own decisions.)

Having weighed the seriousness of my intentions, Caracciolo and Ventura appended the countersignatures necessary for my

---

* Giorgio Almirante (1914–88), leader of the far-right MSI (Movimento Sociale Italiano) since its foundation in 1946.

application to go through. And so, fully aware of what I had done, I received membership card No. 2158861, a hammer-and-sickle on the cover against a red background, and above it a long road leading up to and over the horizon; inside there was the signature of the PCI Secretary, P. Togliatti, and space for the monthly stamps costing 30 lire each.

Also because of that Christian Democrat mysteriously killed near Piazza Vittorio, though certainly not only because of him, the People's Bloc – the joint list of Communists and Socialists, with Garibaldi as its figurehead – did not emerge victorious from the Rome municipal elections. Another, more complex, period was beginning. The world that had miraculously opened up was closing again. The joy was over.

That death in Rome was only the first in a decade that saw massacres of peasants and workers, and new wars both cold and hot. Cesare Pavese understood this early on when he wrote in his diary that *L'Unità* towards the end of the Forties 'was a paper black with headlines like a thunderstorm'. It was black with mourning and defeats, unforeseen because we had not counted on the reactionary denseness of an Italy that was turning Christian Democratic and anti-Communist.

'The road leading me to the PCI is not all downhill', Vittorini had said a year earlier, speaking of 'young people's desperate lives'. He had been referring to the expected revolution that failed to materialize. For those of us in the next generation, who had not fought in the Resistance, there was neither the same disappointment nor the same anger at what some perceived as a betrayal. But in that autumn of 1947, we too sometimes had a gloomy foreboding that the road ahead would be harsh and that our actions would not necessarily be victorious.

I joined the PCI despite this lucidity, or maybe precisely because of what we were then beginning to realize.

The confirmation was not long in coming. A few months later, on 18 April 1948, a night we began with the certainty that 'the Front has won' ended in a bleak dawn in the reception room of the Rome Communist Party on Piazza Sant'Andrea della Valle. Having cycled back and forth from the polling stations with our voting estimates – we didn't trust the official figures – we finally learned of our defeat, bitter, unexpected and inordinate. The secretary, Edoardo D'Onofrio, told us the news, hinting at a historic watershed and appealing for renewed commitment in times when that would be hard indeed.

It was this defeat which really changed me. In the space of a day I lost all my childhood friends, and even my relatives, because a wall had suddenly split the country into two worlds that would remain rigidly apart for decades to come: one in which the PCI was a threatening spectre; and another for which it was an investment in the future, a duty that we thought history had entrusted to us.

Like other comrades, on the day after the defeat of 18 April, I fitted my hammer-and-sickle badge to my collar and displayed it as a defiant challenge. It meant that we were still there, that the game was not over. And three months later, when an attempt was made on Togliatti's life, we went into the streets in a spontaneous general strike such as had never been seen before.

I was taking my first university exam, on 14 July 1948, when Buttaroni – a comrade and the law faculty porter – came and told me the news. We cycled down towards Largo Chigi, which was already filled with people; buses were standing empty in the middle of the road, while lorries and packed old bangers with red flags arrived from the popular districts carrying fierce-looking women: against the Americans, against Christian Democracy, against the police, against the *piselli*.*

I ended up among the 92,000 arrested and charged. It was my first experience of prison, as brief as those that followed. We enjoyed democracy, after all!

THE FIRST IMPACT

In late October 1947, when I became an actual member rather than just a fellow-traveller, I again discovered a new world. This time it was an Italy I had barely glimpsed before, at a few peripheral meetings of the Youth Front.

At the university branch, which had its offices on Corso d'Italia, just off Piazza Fiume, the people were students like me. What was new, however, was the strict discipline that reigned there: meetings every afternoon, and work every morning at La Sapienza – not to attend lectures (I think I only went to one before I graduated, although I passed with honours), but to interrupt them and announce a demonstration, expose an abuse of power, or denounce the killing of workers or farm labourers by the police or the landowners' hired thugs. More and more often we also warned of the new threats to world peace and the dangers of the atom bomb. Many mornings were spent around the statue of Minerva,† or at the faculty, where we watched over our spaces for political activity and

---

* Literally 'peas' – but also slang for 'little pricks', as supporters of Saragat's anti-PCI Socialist grouping were called.

† A statue of Minerva, the Roman goddess of wisdom, is located in the centre of La Sapienza University in Rome.

defended them from almost daily attack by the Fascists (the parents of those in power under Berlusconi).

But there were also cheerier activities, such as the frequent election campaigns for the Inter-Faculty Council or the UNURI (Unione Nazionale Universitaria Rappresentativa Italiana) – the democratic university institutions that were important at the time, and in which we Communists, together with the Socialists in the CUDI (Centro Universitario Democratico Italiano), disputed the still massive dominance of the Right. For years I found myself paired with the Socialist Enrico Manca (a future president of the RAI broadcasting corporation), directly competing with Marco Pannella's pro-Radical UGI (Italian Union of University Students) in the secular anti-Fascist camp.

Other work assigned to me by the branch – its offices were a holy place to which one was admitted after a while, and where Resistance heroes, veterans of Fascist prisons and other legendary figures gathered in flesh and blood – soon came to seem rather more interesting. At first it consisted of political activity in the popular districts of Rome, the 'Red Belt'. We had to catch several buses to get there in the evening, because it was separated even from the outer suburbs by huge areas of uncultivated land that are today cemented over.

In 1948 the Red Belt was overwhelmingly Communist, thanks to an extraordinary effort to rescue it from civic, cultural and political decomposition. Its desperate subproletariat was made up of ex-peasants who had moved to the city to escape the devastation of the Southern war front, tenants evicted from Mussolini's gutted central districts, the unemployed and prostitutes, people living on various expedients, and thieves – all hungry and all crowded together in blocks of flats or makeshift housing erected by the Fascists twenty years earlier. Although my branch secretary, Edoardo D'Onofrio, had long been exiled in the Soviet Union, far from the realities of Italy, he understood that Rome did not have much of a factory working class (apart from the legendary Manzolini and Breda plants), that its proletariat was made up almost entirely of public service workers, and that it was necessary to build the Party among marginal layers scorned by orthodoxy.

Girls like myself were sent to Primavalle or Pietralata to 'educate' the women there – *all* women, including prostitutes, who, we were told, plied their trade out of sheer necessity, and whom we had a duty to instil with a Communist consciousness. This was no simple matter, of course, given that Togliatti was not a populist, and the PCI's paper, *L'Unità* (which we asked them to buy), was mostly written by the elite of intellectuals, with pages of news about events in faraway places, historical background, and arguments to the effect that the desperate multitude should become the national ruling class. Discussions at Party meetings always started from the general world situation, before moving down through Italy and Rome to end up with the water fountain not working at the street corner. This helped to give everyone a sense that they were part of a great international movement marching towards socialism, thereby delivering them from the wretchedness and isolation to which they would otherwise be abandoned.

It was hard at first for us to speak to women in those working-class districts, and harder still for girls to obtain permission – from mothers often surviving 'on the game' – to go out to a meeting or engage in the gymnastic or volleyball activity we organized on nearby wasteland. This got them used to collective life, weaving links that helped to build a new way of looking at the world. But also – anticipating ideas that had not yet occurred to us either – it helped to liberate the body, so that they felt it to be their own and were no longer ashamed to wear shorts. The politics came afterwards, a little at a time. But for us, coming from university, it was an exceptional lesson in politics – today I would say in 'real politics', although at the time I had no idea that it could be any different.

Work in the working-class districts faced me with a variety of human beings I would never otherwise have known; it gave me a rich experience of life which it pains me to see lacking today in my grandchildren, closed as they are in the stifling cage of their class, condemned to mix only with others of their kind, in neighbourhoods and schools that mirror their image back to them. The comrades I met gave me an idea of the world that was no longer abstract, no longer flat and impervious.

They were extraordinary personalities, who gave hour after hour of their day to the collective effort, without even thinking of a reward other than the ideal of human liberation. Elected office, appointments or personal advantage were remote from their horizon. For years I don't think I met any parliamentary deputies or councillors – or if I did, I made no distinction between them and other party activists.

Perhaps my experience was special: we certainly didn't like the Party in the north of the country, which struck us as sullen, rigid and totally workmanlike; we in Rome seemed to have a more human side, buoyant and colourful, which was still disciplined but allowed room for a degree of unconventionality. Luca Canali, the sophisticated Latin scholar, who in those days was secretary of the Trevi-Colonna branch (consisting of fifty cells at street and plant level), has described those Roman comrades in his *Archivo rosso*, a delightful book which, perhaps better than any other, gives an account of what the PCI was really like – just as his next book,

Commiato dal tempo delle bandiere [Farewell to the Age of Flags], charts its decline through the eyes of the same characters, showing how impoverished they became when politics returned to being 'the business of their masters'.

During my first five or six years in the PCI, I did a lot of rank-and-file work in outlying branches and the Roman plain, where the local church would ring its bells if we arrived to make a speech in the central square and women were asked to gather inside behind locked doors to avoid any contact with the devil (proletariat – or, more precisely, subproletariat). We in the Rome organization were distrustful of intellectuals and *L'Unità* journalists: we called them, disdainfully, 'the Navy'. We were the real fighters: the infantry. When my future husband, one of that other aristocratic force, gradually introduced me to its circles, I long felt a sense of unease and estrangement: they seemed anthropologically different, even in their everyday habits. The famous trattorias of central Rome, which have gone down in history as the meeting-places of the postwar intellectual elite, did not exist in my districts on the outskirts of the city. (Let us be clear, though: the ones we despised the most were those we called Narodniks, who wanted to 'turn to the people'. We wanted to *be* the people. And when I discovered that I was not succeeding, that a certain distance remained inside me, I felt myself to be in a state of sin – as if I was not a Communist.)

Later – but not for some time – I began to understand that one could be a Communist even outside a working-class district like Tiburtino III. (In Alfredo Reichlin's recent book, in which he speaks of his 'initiation into Communism', I find all my own motivations and passions, even the same specific references. This means that our generation shared a common 'marrow'.)

186

For years my political activism was uncritical. I accepted the Party's choices and counterchoices without discussing them, because the Party was my moral code. When Stalin died in 1953 – I was in Ferrara for the national congress of the FGCI, which interrupted a session to greet Togliatti on his way by train to Moscow for the funeral – we were all in tears. Why would we have wished Stalin to be in Italy or the Cossacks to water their horses in the fountains of St Peter's? Why did we want Italy to become like the Soviet Union? I don't think any one of us thought it would. Committed to hold back, in ourselves and others, any rebellious temptation, we threw ourselves, as we were asked to, into building the democratic forms of the Italian road to socialism; the USSR was 'the concrete symbol that another world was possible', the unspoken reserve which implied our irreducible otherness vis-à-vis the system in which we were living. It was this which gave us sufficient distance to imagine a different future – an ideal horizon, then, not an actual political project. It has been called 'two-faced', but what it involved was not two strategies but a double truth: the one expressing caution with regard to the other's possible illusions. In a way, the Soviet Union was the indispensable hinterland guaranteeing that the democratic venture on which we had embarked would not be integrated into the existing system.

Today, if I am asked what was the key reason for my choice of Communism, I give the banal answer that it was my way of giving up navel-gazing; the PCI was the means for me to open my eyes and look at the world, to stop feeling useless in the face of injustices. Above all, though, it enabled me to avoid remaining stupid, as I would have if I had not left my native ghetto and had the possibility of sharing with various comrades the finest of all passions: the ambition to change the world.

I have never regretted my decision to join the PCI in 1947, at the end of a trajectory that began on 25 July 1943 in Riccione and gradually took me to the Roman Party organization at Piazza Sant'Andrea della Valle.

It is not that I was unaware of the price: indeed, this may have seemed higher at the time than the one we were eventually asked to pay. Giving up the cosy life of my childhood certainly did not matter to me at all. If anything weighed on my mind, it was the knowledge that I would be excluded from official society. It was like entering a kind of clandestine existence. But that too had its fascination.

At any event, the exclusion did not last long. By the late Fifties, the PCI's status in the world had changed and newspapers, universities and even drawing-rooms had begun to open up to Communists. They were no longer refused passports, and only rarely went to prison. (For me and thirty-two building workers there was a sequel in extra time, as it were: two months in Rebibbia prison for a set-to in Piazza Santi Apostoli that was later shown to have been a provocation staged by the clandestine CIA-backed Gladio organization. That was in 1963 – the last flick of the tail by the centre-right government during the Antonio Segni presidency.)

That PCI membership card issued in 1947, No. 2158861, is still in my possession, together with all the others from my career as a Communist: a total of twenty-four up to 1970, when I was expelled in January because of the *Manifesto* heresy. The decisive vote took place in my Party branch, Ponte Milvio, which had to comply in the end, having previously refused to obey the request from the Federal Control Commission; by a curious stroke of history Giuliano Ferrara was among those who took part in the act. I also still have my rough membership cards of the proto-organization that called itself Il

Manifesto, and of the actual party that we went on to found: the PdUP (Party of Proletarian Unity). This later decided, at a special congress in late 1984, to dissolve and re-enter the PCI, in response to an invitation that Enrico Berlinguer extended to us shortly before his death. The questions that divided us – the Prague Spring, the events of 1968 – are now behind us, he said.

We rejoined with full honours. In the joint statement also signed by PCI secretary Alessandro Natta – a document unprecedented in the history of Communist parties – it was said that splits sometimes serve a purpose by deepening debate.

When I returned to my old Ponte Milvio branch to receive my 1985 membership card, the secretary was in a bit of a quandary. How was he to complete 'joined the PCI in ...'? 1947 or 1985? What attitude should he have to the fifteen missing years that followed my expulsion in 1970? In the end he laughed – times had changed – and gave me a hug. 'It's obvious', he said, inserting '1947' without further ado.

As we all know, there was not much longer to go. After six more cards, the seventh – issued in 1991 – would be the last in the history of the PCI.

And then. That is another story. But the fact remains that my decision back in 1947 gave me eyes and ears with which to get to know my country. I think I did the right thing. Far from regretting it, I today have an overwhelming nostalgia for that party, with all its defects. It will be said that it is nostalgia for a period rather than a party. Of course, there's that too. But without that party the period would not have been the same.

INDEX

191

INDEX

Index

INDEX